GMAT®

Critical Reasoning

GRAIL

Copyright, Legal Notice and Disclaimer:

Aristotle Prep CR Grail

10-digit International Standard Book Number: **9350872854**

13-digit International Standard Book Number: **978-9350872857**

Publisher: Aristotle Prep

Contents

Introduction

Critical Reasoning (CR), even though part of the verbal section, does not really test you on your grasp of the English language. As the name suggests, this section is actually a test of your reasoning skills. The only *verbal* aspect is that you have to know enough English to be able to understand the meaning of the arguments and the options given to you. The *critical* part of Critical Reasoning is that you have to read the question stem and the options very carefully. If you even miss a single word such as *some*, you could end up with a completely incorrect answer.

To most students, Critical Reasoning is the easiest of the three question types tested on the verbal section of the GMAT. Even if it is indeed so, it makes sense to maximise your accuracy in this section so as to compensate for the slightly lower accuracy rate that you may have in the Sentence Correction and Reading Comprehension sections. This book will help you do just that.

Remember that, unlike Sentence Correction, Critical Reasoning will not require you to go through myriad rules and exceptions to the rules and further exceptions to these exceptions! Critical Reasoning involves the use of just a few basic concepts and approaches to different question types. This book will take you through all of these, after which it will all boil down to practice.

This book will first take you through the basics of Critical Reasoning before moving on to discuss in detail the various question types that are commonly tested on the GMAT. The book will then take you through some common argument structures and some red herring terms that you should look out for in order to eliminate incorrect options. Once you've gone through all the concepts, the book offers a 100 question practice set to test how well you have understood these concepts. Finally the last section of the book will summarise all the concepts discussed in this book, making it easy for you to quickly revise everything.

One thing we have consciously tried to avoid is making the entire process of understanding arguments too mechanical by the use of symbols/diagrams. Instead our stress throughout this book will be on understanding the meaning of the arguments by looking for different signalling words and latching on to subtle hints provided in the arguments.

We hope that you will find this book useful in your quest to achieve a high GMAT score. As always please send us your thoughts on this book at feedback@aristotleprep.com.

Good luck!

SECTION 1

Basics of Critical Reasoning

Basics of Critical Reasoning

Every Critical Reasoning question that you see on the GMAT will have three parts to it:

1. **The Stimulus** – This is the main body of the argument

2. **The Question Stem** – This is the one or two lines in the middle that actually tell you what you have to do – find the assumption, strengthen, weaken, etc. In *Provide a Logical Conclusion* question type, this tends to be before the stimulus.

3. **The Options** – Each question will have five options from which you will need to identify the correct one.

The stimulus will usually appear in two forms – as an argument or as several statements of facts. To understand the difference between the two, let's look at what makes up an argument. Most arguments will have the following three parts – *Conclusion, Evidence, and Assumption.*

Conclusion, Evidence, and Assumption

Let's try to understand these terms with an example:

> *People don't like to visit the Evergreen wildlife park in the rainy season. This year the park authorities have reconstructed all the roads inside the park, so people will like to visit the Evergreen Park in the rainy reason this year.*

Conclusion – This is the point of the argument and answers the question *What* i.e. what is the argument basically stating - *that people would like to visit the Evergreen Wildlife park in the rainy season this year.*

Conclusions usually follow signalling words such as *thus, so, hence, therefore, etc.* In case there are no such words in the argument, try to paraphrase the entire argument in one sentence. This sentence would almost always be the conclusion of the argument.

Evidence – While the Conclusion tells you *What* the argument is saying, the Evidence tells you *Why* the argument is concluding what it is concluding. So in the above argument, why does the author conclude that people will like to visit the Evergreen Park this year? Because the park authorities have reconstructed all the roads inside the park, so this becomes your evidence.

Evidence usually follows signalling words such as *because, since, as a result of, etc.*

So the conclusion tells you the ***what*** of the argument and the evidence tells you the ***why*** of the argument. Another way of looking at conclusion and evidence is that a conclusion will almost always be *an opinion* whereas the evidence will almost always be *a fact*. In the above argument it is a fact that the roads have been reconstructed but it is the author's opinion that people will like to visit the Evergreen Park this year.

Assumption - Now, going back to the above argument, notice that from the given evidence we cannot necessarily arrive at the stated conclusion. The argument only states that people don't want to visit the Evergreen Park during the rainy season; it never states why people don't like to do so. So the author *assumes* that the only reason people don't like to visit the park is because of the poor road conditions within the park. If this is not assumed then the argument will fall apart.

For example, if the real reason why people do not visit the Evergreen Park was the fact that there are hardly any animals in the park, then even if the roads were made of velvet people will not visit the park because bad roads was not the reason for people not visiting the park in the first place. So, for the author to conclude that people will want to visit the park this year, he has to assume that the only reason people did not visit the park earlier was the poor road condition inside the park.

So, now that you know what components make up an argument, let's look at the relation among these. All arguments will have the following structure:

EVIDENCE + ASSUMPTION = CONCLUSION

In essence you can think of the assumption as unstated evidence or as a bridge between the evidence and the conclusion. If this bridge collapses, then you cannot arrive at the conclusion from the given evidence.

Here it is very important to note that the assumption is always *unstated* evidence i.e. it will never be written in the argument. It has to be assumed in the mind. So in a *find an assumption* question, if one of the options restates what is already mentioned in the argument, then this cannot be the assumption.

So, to summarize, with reference to the above argument:

> ***The Conclusion*** - people would like to visit the Evergreen Wildlife Park in the rainy season this year
>
> ***The Evidence*** - the park authorities have reconstructed the roads within the park.
>
> ***The Assumption*** – the only reason people do not visit the Evergreen National park in the rainy season is because of the poor roads within the park

One mistake students make is to assume that the last sentence of the argument will always be the conclusion. Nothing could be farther from the truth. The conclusion can be at the beginning of the argument, in the middle of the argument, or at the end of the argument.

Argument with conclusion at the beginning:

> *The Wind Wane project is an excellent one for Sihora County.* The project will generate employment for the local population and also provide the residents with energy at low costs. In addition it will also lead to the opening up of new schools and colleges in Sihora County.

Argument with conclusion in the middle:

> The Wind Wane project will generate employment for the local population in Sihora County and also provide the residents with energy at low costs. *So, the Wind Wane project is an excellent one for Sihora County.* In addition, the project will also lead to the opening up of new schools and colleges in Sihora County.

Argument with conclusion at the end:

> The Wind Wane project will generate employment for the local population in Sihora County and also provide the residents with energy at low costs. In addition it will also lead to the opening up of new schools and colleges in Sihora County. *So, the Wind Wane project is an excellent one for Sihora County.*

So if the conclusion can be anywhere in an argument, how do you identify it. The answer is simple – by applying the *What and Why method* we discussed earlier.

What is the author saying (Conclusion) – The Wind Wane project is an excellent one for Sihora County

Why is the author saying so (Evidence) – Because the Wind Wane project will generate employment for the local population in Sihora County, provide them with energy at low costs, and also lead to the opening up of new schools and colleges in Sihora County.

So there you have your conclusion and evidence. The *What and Why* method is especially useful because it will actually force you to understand the meaning of the argument as a whole.

Stimulus with a set of Facts

As stated earlier, some question stimulus' will contain arguments but some may just contain statements of facts without any conclusion.

For example

> The sale of automobiles has increased by more than 100% in Vino city in the last one year. Out of this increase, more than 70% comprise Multi utility vehicles and Sports utility vehicles. Hatchbacks comprise the rest of the 30% sales figure.

As you can see the above stimulus just gives you some facts or data without arriving at any conclusion as such.

So a stimulus can be in the form of an argument or it may just comprise a set of facts. This will to a large extent be determined by the question type that you get. For example, in a *find the assumption* question the stimulus will always be in the form of an argument and for an *Explain the Contradiction* question the stimulus will always contain facts.

Initial Steps to approach Critical Reasoning questions on the GMAT

- Always start by reading the stimulus. Some students prefer reading the question stem first but to us it's a waste of time because you'll read the question stem, then read the stimulus, and then invariably read the question stem again.

- Read the stimulus critically. Pay attention to every word. In the end summarize everything in your own words. If the stimulus is in the form of an argument be clear on *What* the stimulus is stating and *Why* it is stating so.

- Read the Question stem and use the strategy to tackle that particular question type, as described in the subsequent chapters of this book

- You should take an average of two minutes to answer each Critical Reasoning question. This is an average figure, so some questions may take you longer and some may be completed in less than two minutes

SECTION 1

Critical Reasoning Question Types

The GMAT is a structured test so it will test you on a predictable pattern. In Critical Reasoning, there are certain question types that are tested again and again. We'll be looking at each of these question types in this section of the book.

The questions tested on the GMAT can be broadly divided into the following eight types:

GMAT Critical Reasoning Question Types

1. Find the Assumption Questions
    a. Useful to know/evaluate Questions
2. Strengthen Questions
3. Weaken Questions
4. Identify the Flaw Questions
    a. Vulnerable to the objection/criticism Questions
5. Inference Questions
    a. Must be true Questions
6. Explain a Contradiction Questions
7. Provide a Logical Conclusion Questions
8. Miscellaneous Questions
    a. Bold Faced Questions
    b. Main Point Questions
    c. Parallel Reasoning Questions

Some question types can be worded in different ways; for example an assumption question can sometimes be given in the form of a 'useful to know/evaluate questions' but the underlying objective is to identify the assumption correctly. Similarly instead of asking you to directly identify a flaw in the argument, the question can also ask you what criticism would the argument be most vulnerable to.

Out of these question types, the five that will be tested most often are *Assumption, Strengthen, Weaken, Inference and Explain* questions. Around 70% of the questions on the test will comprise these five question types.

Let's take a look at each of these question types in detail over the next few chapters.

Assumption Questions

Assumption Questions

Assumption is the most important of all the Critical Reasoning concepts/question types. This is because assumption will give you the answer to five question types – *Find the Assumption questions (but of course), Evaluate the argument questions, Strengthen questions, Weaken questions, and Flaw questions.* We will see the connection between assumptions and each of these question types in later chapters but first let's take a look at assumptions themselves.

As we discussed in the previous chapter, an assumption is basically the unstated evidence that must be true for the argument's conclusion to be true. The most important thing to keep in mind while trying to arrive at the assumption is that the author's conclusion is true, even if it is the most absurd of conclusions. A lot of the times the problem students face is that they end up questioning the logic or validity of the author' argument. Leave that thought process for Weaken or Flaw questions. For Assumption questions you must take the author's conclusion to be absolutely one hundred percent true.

So, if the author concludes that aliens will arrive next week then you must agree with this fact; only then will you be able to arrive at the assumption correctly. For example, in this case one assumption may be that the shiny object in the sky is a space ship commanded by aliens. While it is extremely unlikely that the GMAT will give you an argument such as the alien one, the reason we picked such an extreme example is to drive home the point that whatever the author states has to be taken as the truth by you. Never question the conclusion; instead focus your energies on identifying what else needs to be true for the author's conclusion to be true and you would have arrived at the assumption.

Over the last six years, most of the students in Tupac city have regularly attended colleges in the neighbouring Mekon city to pursue their graduate degrees. However, according to a recent change in the education policies of Mekon city, the colleges in Mekon city are expected to increase their fees to almost the same level as those charged by colleges in Tupac city. Therefore it can be safely concluded that colleges in Tupac city will see a surge in the number of students enrolling with them to pursue their graduate degrees

Which of the following is an assumption on which the argument depends?

A. The teachers at colleges in Mekon city are generally considered superior to those at colleges in Tupac city

B. Tupac city does not have good quality colleges

C. The low fees charged by colleges at Mekon city is the primary reason why students from Tupac city move to these colleges

D. Students who study at colleges in Tupac city do not perform better than those who study at colleges in Mekon city

E. Mekon city does not have more colleges than Tupac city

Always start an assumption question by paraphrasing the conclusion and the evidence.

Conclusion (What is the author saying) – that there will be a surge in the enrolments at colleges in Tupac city

Evidence (Why is the author saying this) – because students in Tupac city who earlier used to move to Mekon city to pursue their graduate degrees will now not do so as the colleges in Mekon city will charge them the same fees as the colleges in Tupac city do.

Note that that conclusion is an opinion of the author but the evidence is a fact because the colleges in Mekon city are definitely looking at increasing their fees.

The Importance of Predicting the Assumption

On assumption questions, it always helps if you already have a rough answer in mind before you look at the options as this can prevent you from getting confused between or among very close choices.

For example, given the above conclusion and evidence set, in order to arrive at the conclusion from the given evidence what must the author of the argument be assuming?

The author must be assuming that the low fees charged by colleges in Mekon city is the single most important factor why students from Tupac city have been moving to colleges in Mekon city. If he does not assume this, the argument will fall apart.

For example, if students have been shifting to Mekon city because the teachers in Mekon city colleges are better than those at Tupac city colleges then, even if the fees at colleges in Mekon City go up, students will keep on moving to Mekon city because the reason for the shift is the better quality of teachers.

So for the author's conclusion to be true, he has to assume that the only reason students have been shifting to colleges in Mekon city is the low fees charged by colleges in Mekon city. Option (C) states this best and hence is the correct answer.

However, just to get more clarity, let's take a look at the other options as well:

A. As we saw above, this fact actually weakens the argument because in this case the students will keep on shifting to colleges in Mekon City

B. Quality of colleges is outside the scope of the argument because the argument is only concerned with the fees charged by colleges. In fact, just like option (A), (B) could also weaken the argument by suggesting that lower fees is not the reason why students might be moving to colleges in Mekon city

C. The correct answer

D. This may or may not be the case but doesn't have to be the case for the author's conclusion to be true

E. The number of colleges in each city is irrelevant to the argument

The Denial/Negation Rule for Assumption questions

On Assumption questions, in case you are confused between two or more options, an effective way to eliminate incorrect options is by applying the Negation rule to the answer choices. The Negation or Denial rule is based on the principle that the assumption has to be true for the argument's conclusion to be true. As a corollary to this, if the assumption is denied or negated, then the argument must fall apart.

Hence, under the Negation rule, all you do is try to deny or negate each option and check whether the argument's conclusion can still be true. If it can be true then this option is not the assumption. Likewise if denying an option makes the conclusion fall apart then this option has to be the assumption.

Let's try the denial rule with each of the options in the Tupac city vs. Mekon city question discussed above:

A. The teachers at colleges in Mekon city are generally NOT considered far superior to those at colleges in Tupac city

   Negation this option does not help in any way because the argument is never about the quality of teachers in the first place. In its original wording this option was weakening the argument, now it is not doing anything.

B. Tupac city does ~~not~~ have good quality colleges

   Since this option already contains the word *not*, the ideal way to negate this is to remove the *not*. Again this does not explain why students have been shifting in the first place and quality of colleges is never the issue anyway.

C. The low fees charged by colleges at Mekon city is NOT the primary reason why students from Tupac city move to these colleges

   Negating this option definitely makes the argument fall apart because in this case the students will keep on shifting to colleges in Mekon City even after the increase in fees. Then, there will be no surge in enrolments at colleges in Tupac city. So this option has to be the assumption.

D. Students who study at colleges in Tupac city ~~do not~~ perform better than those who study at colleges in Mekon city

   Again strike out the *do not* from this option to negate it. Like option B, if this were to be the case then the students wouldn't have been shifting from Tupac city to Mekon city in the first place

E. Mekon city does ~~not~~ have more colleges than Tupac city

   The number of colleges in either city is irrelevant to our argument.

So you can see the denial or the negation rule can come in very handy when you are confused between options. However ***don't apply this rule on all the five options*** and waste your time. Two or three options can usually easily be eliminated; apply this rule to the remaining options.

Active and Passive Assumptions

Active assumptions are those assumptions that actively support the argument. These are the predictions you come up with when you are trying to pre-phrase an assumption. Active assumptions must be true for the argument to be true.

However, do notice the fact that the moment you assume that something must be true in an argument, you automatically assume that the other possibilities must NOT be true. It is these other possibilities that we call Passive Assumptions.

For example, in the Tupac city vs. Mekon city argument discussed earlier, the moment the author assumes that the primary reason students have been moving to colleges in Mekon city is the low fees charged by these colleges, he automatically assumes that other factors (such as better quality of teachers or better infrastructure) cannot be the reason for this shift. So the following can also be the assumptions in that argument:

- The better quality of teachers at colleges in Mekon city is *not* the primary reason why students have been shifting to colleges in Mekon city

- The better infrastructure at colleges in Mekon city is *not* the primary reason why students have been shifting to colleges in Mekon city

- The large number of clubs and entertainment centres in Mekon city is *not* the primary reason why students have been shifting to colleges in Mekon city

Notice that denying any of the above assumptions will make the original argument fall apart.

As you can see we can keep on making as many passive assumptions as we want. This is the biggest difference between active and passive assumptions. There can only be one active assumption in an argument but there can be several passive assumptions. It is precisely for this reason that you cannot predict a passive assumption whereas you can predict an active assumption.

You may have noticed that all the passive assumptions written above contain the word ***not***. This is the best way to identify passive assumptions since by definition they will always contain some negating word, most often *not*.

Let's look at one final example to understand active and passive assumptions.

> It takes four hours to cover the distance between Aston and Torin cities by bus. John has boarded a bus at Aston city that is scheduled to depart for Torin city at 10:00 a.m. If the bus departs on its correct time, John will reach Torin city well in time to attend his interview scheduled for 4:00pm that afternoon.
>
> **Active Assumption** – The bus will not get delayed on the way from Aston to Torin.
>
> **Passive Assumptions**
>
> - The bus will not have a flat tie or all four flat tires
> - The bus will not be struck by lightning
> - The bus will not be attacked by gunmen
> - The bus driver will not decide to go to some other city, etc.

So the active assumption gives you one general assumption and the passive assumption gives you several, each of which refutes the possibility of the active assumption not being true.

Author's note: *Do not get unnecessarily confused between active and passive assumptions since on the GMAT nobody will ask you to distinguish between or identify the two. Just know that there is something like a passive assumption so that when you see it on a question you don't end up eliminating it immediately because it may actually be the correct answer.*

So try this question then:

> Eating unhygienic food always results in cases of stomach infection or food poisoning. Dominic is currently suffering from food poisoning, so he must have eaten unhygienic food in the last few days.

Which of the following is an assumption on which the argument depends?

(A) Eating unhygienic food will most definitely lead to food poisoning

(B) Dominic does not have a weak immune system that makes him prone to food poisoning

(C) Dominic can make out the difference between hygienic and unhygienic food

(D) Eating unhygienic food is the only way to get food poisoning

(E) Unhygienic food contains harmful bacteria and other pathogens that lead to food poisoning

The Conclusion – Dominic must have eaten unhygienic food in the last few days

The Evidence – Eating unhygienic food always leads to food poisoning and Dominic is currently suffering from food poisoning

The Assumption – The argument states that eating unhygienic food will always lead to a person getting food poisoning. There can be no question about this fact since this is given to us as evidence. However the argument never states that this is the *only* way to get food poisoning. There could also be other ways of getting food poisoning such as drinking impure water or eating hygienic food with dirty hands.

So for the author's conclusion to be true, he has to assume that the only way to contract food poisoning is by consuming unhygienic food. (D) states this best and should be the correct answer.

Let's look at the other options as well;

(A) This is clearly stated in the argument so cannot be the assumption. In fact this is part of the evidence. Remember that an assumption will never be stated, it is always assumed

(B) This option is a trap because it has been worded in the form of a passive assumption (notice the use of the word *not*). However even if Dominic does have a weak immune system, he may still have contracted food poisoning from some source other than unhygienic food.

(C) Whether Dominic is able to make out this difference is irrelevant. In fact it is possible that he could not make out this difference, which is why he ended up having unhygienic food in the first place

(D) The Correct Answer

(E) How unhygienic food leads to food poisoning is not the concern of the argument.

The following can be Passive Assumptions in the argument:

- Drinking impure water cannot lead to food poisoning, (*because if it can then maybe this is how Dominic contracted food poisoning and not by consuming unhygienic food)*
- Eating with dirty hands cannot lead to food poisoning, (*because if it can then maybe this is how Dominic contracted food poisoning and not by consuming unhygienic food)*

The wording of Assumption Questions

Assumption questions most often directly ask you to identify the assumption in the argument. However sometimes they can be worded in the form of *must be true* questions.

Here is an example:

> *Which of the following must be true for the above argument to be true?*

This shouldn't come as a surprise because conceptually an assumption must be true for an argument to be valid.

You'll see a variation of this when we discuss *Inference questions* subsequently in this book.

How to Approach Assumption Questions

1. Read the argument and be clear on the evidence and the conclusion
2. Know that since this is an assumption question, there has to be some piece of evidence missing from the argument

3. Try to predict this missing piece of evidence. In a *Find the Assumption* question, you must always have an answer in mind before you look at the options

4. Eliminate two or three options because they definitely appear to be incorrect. Possible wrong answer choices can be those that are outside the scope of the argument, that repeat what is stated in the argument, or that can be inferred from the argument.

5. If stuck between two or more options try the denial or negation rule

Evaluate the Argument Questions

Evaluate the Argument Questions

Evaluate the Argument questions will ask you to identify that option which can best help you verify whether what is stated in the argument is true or not. Since all arguments contain assumptions, the only way to evaluate how logical an argument is, is to verify whether its assumption is true or false. If the assumption is true, then the argument is definitely logical and vice versa.

So in an Evaluate the Argument question, you are being tested on Assumptions in a roundabout manner.

A recent nationwide survey of dementia patients revealed an interesting fact – almost all of the patients surveyed were more than 70 years of age and watched more than six hours of television every day. So, people who are more than 70 years of age should avoid watching more than six hours of television everyday to avoid getting afflicted with dementia.

Which of the following would it be most useful to determine in order to evaluate the argument?

(A) Whether people less than 70 years of age can also get afflicted with dementia

(B) Whether there are some visible symptoms of dementia, thereby making it easier to identify such cases

(C) Whether being afflicted with dementia makes people want to watch more television

(D) Whether regular therapy and medicines can reverse the onset of dementia

(E) Whether there can be some additional cause of dementia, in addition to watching more than six hours of television every day

Since the stimulus is in the form of an argument, let's break it down into its components.

Conclusion (What is the author saying) – that people who are more than 70 years of age should avoid watching more than six hours of television in one day

Evidence (Why is the author saying this) – because, according to the results of a survey, most dementia patients were more than 70 years of age and watched more than six hours of television every day.

Thus the study basically concludes that the presence of two things together (dementia and watching more than six hours of television every day) implies that one is the cause of the other.

However, it is also possible that this may just be a coincidence and that there actually could be some other cause of dementia. Or it is also possible that it is because people are afflicted with dementia that makes them want to watch more than six hours of television every day. The answer to these questions will basically help us better evaluate the argument.

Do notice that both of the scenarios mentioned above are actually assumptions in the argument so, in order to evaluate the argument, all you need to do is to identify whether the assumption being made in the argument will be true or not.

Assumption (The unstated Premise) – There can be two assumptions in this argument – first that the correlation described in the stimulus is actually a cause and effect relation and second, that even if this correlation is indeed a cause and effect relation, it is watching TV that is the cause of dementia and not vice versa i.e. dementia is the cause of watching TV. (C) states the second one of these and should be the correct answer.

Let's also look at the other options for more clarity:

(A) The question is not the age at which people get dementia but whether there is a causal link between watching television and getting afflicted with dementia

(B) Again the symptoms of dementia are irrelevant to the connection between dementia and watching television for a certain number of hours

(C) The correct answer. If true, this fact will strengthen the argument and if false, it will weaken the argument

(D) The cure for dementia is not the concern of the argument

(E) This doesn't help us ascertain whether there is a causal link between watching television and getting afflicted with dementia

So *Evaluate the argument* questions will ask you to identify whether the assumption in the argument will be true or not. The options for these questions will usually either be in the form of questions or will start with the word *whether*. The correct answer will be the option that, if true, strengthens the argument and if false, weakens the argument.

So try this question then:

> Company X and Company Y are in the business of manufacturing memory cards. Company X sells twice as many memory cards as does Company Y and Company X also has fewer employees than Company Y does. So Company X must be making more profits than Company Y.
>
> Which of the following options best helps to evaluate the argument?
>
> (A) Whether there are any other companies who manufacture memory cards in addition to Company X and Company Y
>
> (B) Whether both the companies pay similar average salaries to their employees
>
> (C) Whether Company X will be able to sustain its high sales in the future
>
> (D) Whether the memory cards of the two companies have similar storage capacities
>
> (E) Whether Company X is likely to hire more employees in the near future

The Conclusion – Company X must be making more profits than Company Y

The Evidence – Company X sells many more memory cards than does Company Y. Also Company X has fewer employees (so its overall salary cost will be lower than that for Company Y)

The Assumption – For this question one can come up with several assumptions.

- the selling price of the memory cards of the two companies is the same
- the salaries that the two companies pay to their employees is the same

- company X does not incur any extra expenditure on advertising, sales promotion, etc

So the knowledge of any of the above listed points will make it easier for us to evaluate the given argument. B points out one of these (the average salaries at the two companies) and should be the correct answer.

Let's look at the other options:

(A) The conclusion only talks about the relative position of Company X with reference to Company Y. The existence of other companies (who could be better or worse than these two) is irrelevant

(B) The Correct Answer

(C) The conclusion talks about the present so what may happen in the future is irrelevant

(D) The storage capacities of the memory cards do not matter because the final sales figure will not change because of this fact

(E) Like option C, the conclusion talks about the present so what may happen in the future is irrelevant

How to Approach Evaluate the Argument Questions

1. Read the argument and be clear on the evidence and the conclusion

2. Know that an *Evaluate the Argument* question is indirectly asking you to identify the assumption, so try to predict this assumption. You may be able to come up with several of them

3. Look at each option and eliminate. Remember that the correct answer will strengthen the argument, if true, and weaken the argument, if false.

Strengthen

Questions

Strengthen Questions

Strengthen questions, as the name suggests, will require you to strengthen whatever it is that an argument is stating. However, do keep in mind that strengthen does not mean to confirm an argument. Even if an option can provide a small point in favour of the argument it is strengthening the argument. Similarly even if an option can remove a small doubt from your mind about the argument, it is again strengthening the argument.

Notice that to strengthen a stimulus, it is imperative that the stimulus have a conclusion. So strengthen questions will always contain a stimulus that is in the form of an argument.

Of all the laptops available for sale in Ireland, those manufactured by Ivy Infotech must have the fastest processors. Over the last six months Ivy Infotech has sold three times as many laptops as its closest competitor. Additionally Ivy Infotech's order books are full for the next 12 months.

Which of the following options, if true, most strengthens the argument?

A. Ivy Infotech is the oldest manufacturer of laptops in Ireland

B. Ivy Infotech has the largest market share in laptop sales in Ireland for the past five years

C. Ivy Infotech sources its processors from the company which is the world's biggest manufacturer of laptop processors

D. All the laptops available for sale in Ireland are same in every aspect except for their processors

E. The Irish populace prefers laptops with faster processors

Since this is a strengthen question, you know that the stimulus will be worded in the form of an argument. So the first step is to identify the conclusion and the evidence of this argument.

Conclusion (What is the argument stating) – Laptops manufactured by Ivy Infotech have the fastest processors.

Evidence (Why is the argument stating this) – Because Ivy Infotech has sold the maximum number of laptops in the last six months in Ireland.

But does this make sense? Can't there be some other plausible reason why the people in Ireland are buying Ivy Infotech's laptops?

Maybe these laptops have a very sleek design, maybe they have a very long batter life, or maybe they are the cheapest laptops in the market. There can be several other reasons (other than fast processors) why the Irish are buying laptops manufactured by Ivy Infotech. This brings us to the assumption. Remember that since the stimulus is in the form of an argument, it must contain an assumption.

Assumption (the unstated evidence) – So let's try to predict the assumption. It will be something on the lines of 'the only difference among the different laptops available in Ireland is the speed of the processor; the laptops are the same in every other aspect', because then if the people are still buying Ivy Infotech's laptops then these laptops must have the fastest processors, else people would be buying some other company's laptops.

Strengthener – So now that we have identified the conclusion, the evidence, and the assumption, the option that best tells us that the assumption is true has to strengthen the argument. (D) does this best and should be the correct answer.

For clarity, let's also take a look at the other options:

A. The argument is only concerned with processor speeds accounting for high sales. It has got nothing to do with how old a company is.

B. Again this option doesn't tell us why Ivy Infotech has the largest market share. Is it the processor speed or some other reason?

C. Very well but it is possible that the other competitors of Ivy Infotech also source their processors from this same company

D. The correct answer. If the only difference among the laptops is the processor speed and if people are still buying laptops manufactured by Ivy Infotech, then these laptops must have the fastest processors.

E. The option uses the word 'prefers' which doesn't tell you anything. You could prefer flying by a private jet to flying by a commercial airline but you mostly still have to fly by a commercial airline. So the Irish could prefer laptops with faster chips but might buy some other laptop which has a slightly slower processor but a much longer battery life or which is much cheaper in price.

Strengtheners and Assumptions

Did you notice something interesting in the above question – the correct answer is almost a paraphrase of the assumption that we had predicted earlier i.e. the strengthener is the same as the assumption. If you think about it, conceptually this has to be the case. An assumption is unstated evidence that strengthens an argument so if this unstated evidence is stated in the form of an option, then it will obviously strengthen the argument. So a strengthener will either be the assumption itself or it will supply some evidence that will make it more likely for the assumption to be true.

Thus the answer to a strengthen question will a lot of the times be the assumption, though you may not consciously realize this all the time.

Active and Passive Strengtheners

Since strengtheners follow from the assumption, it is but obvious that, just like we had active and passive assumptions, we'll also have active and passive strengtheners. An active strengthener will give you a positive point i.e. a point in favour of the argument whereas a passive strengthener will remove one or more of the negative points from the argument.

The following can be some passive strengtheners for the Ivy Infotech example:

- Sleek design is not the reason why the Irish are buying Ivy Infotech's laptops

- A longer battery life is not the reason why the Irish are buying Ivy Infotech's laptops

- The fact that Ivy Infotech's laptops are the cheapest laptops available in the market is not the reason why the Irish are buying Ivy Infotech's laptops

Notice that all these passive strengtheners again use the word *not*, just as passive assumptions do.

So a passive strengthener, in essence, removes a doubt from your mind about the argument whereas an active strengthener gives you some supporting point in favour of the argument

Always strengthen the connection between the Evidence and the Conclusion

While strengthen questions are generally easy, there is one folly that you must guard against – you must, at all times, try to strengthen the connection between the evidence and the conclusion. Never strengthen the conclusion in isolation (even if the argument asks you to strengthen the conclusion).

> I read in the newspaper this morning that in the last one month 20 children have been kidnapped in Sodham County, when they stepped out of their house alone at night. So I conclude that if you are a child

staying in Sodham County, it is unsafe for you to step out alone at night.

Which of the following two options strengthens my argument?

1. I read this article in a newspaper that is a very trustworthy newspaper known for its honest credible reporting.

2. Two child kidnappers, who have recently been released from prison, have been seen loitering around in Sodham County at night over the last month.

While a lot of you may have gone with option two as the correct answer, it is in fact incorrect. Why am I concluding that if you are a child in Sodham County it is unsafe for you to step out alone at night? Not because I know something about the child kidnappers, but because I read something in the newspaper.

Another person could very well come and tell me that the newspaper is known for false reporting and for sensationalising things, facts which would weaken my argument. The opposite facts, as stated in option one, will then obviously strengthen my argument because my evidence is the newspaper article.

So the takeaway is that you always try to strengthen the link between the evidence and the conclusion. The evidence is there for a purpose and you must make use of it.

How to Approach Strengthen Questions

1. Read the argument and be clear on the evidence and the conclusion

2. Try to predict the assumption because the strengthener will, in some way, be linked to this

3. Go through the options and eliminate those that weaken the argument or are otherwise outside the scope of the argument

4. Remember to take into consideration the evidence as well; don't just strengthen the conclusion in isolation

Weaken

Questions

Weaken Questions

Weaken questions, as the name suggests, will require you to weaken or raise doubts about whatever it is that an argument is stating. In that sense these are the exact opposite of Strengthen questions that you saw in the previous chapter.

Do keep in mind that weaken does not mean to negate an argument. Even if an option can raise a small doubt in your mind about the validity of the argument, it is weakening the argument. Similarly if an option removes a strengthener from an argument, it is again weakening the argument.

Notice that to weaken a stimulus, it is imperative that the stimulus have a conclusion. So weaken questions will always contain a stimulus that is in the form of an argument.

For conceptual clarity, let's look at the same example that we saw in the previous chapter but with different options.

Of all the laptops available for sale in Ireland, laptops manufactured by Ivy Infotech must have the fastest processors. Over the last six months Ivy Infotech has sold three times as many laptops as its closest competitor. Additionally Ivy Infotech's order books are full for the next 12 months.

Which of the following options, if true, most weakens the argument?

A. Ivy Infotech was severely criticised last year for manufacturing laptops with slow processors

B. Apart from laptops, Ivy Infotech also manufactures desktops and tablets, sales of which have declined drastically in the last six months

C. At the same time last year, Ivy Infotech had sold 60% more laptops than it has this year

D. All the laptop manufacturers in Ireland, including Ivy Infotech, source their processors from the same company

E. Due to production bottlenecks, the production of laptops by Ivy Infotech's rival companies has fallen by more than 60% in the last six months

Since this is a weaken question, you know that the stimulus will be worded in the form of an argument. So the first step is to identify the conclusion and the evidence of this argument.

Conclusion (What is the argument stating) – Laptops manufactured by Ivy Infotech have the fastest processors.

Evidence (Why is the argument stating this) – Because Ivy Infotech has sold the maximum number of laptops in the last six months in Ireland.

But does this make sense? Can't there be some other plausible reason why the people in Ireland are buying Ivy Infotech's laptops? Maybe these laptops have a very sleek design, maybe they have a very long batter life, or maybe they are the cheapest laptops in the market. There can be several other reasons (other than fast processors) why the Irish are buying laptops manufactured by Ivy Infotech. This brings us to the assumption. Remember that since the stimulus is in the form of an argument, it must contain an assumption.

Assumption (the unstated evidence) – So let's try to predict the assumption. It will be something on the lines of 'the only difference among the different laptops available in Ireland is the speed of the processor; the laptops are the same in every other aspect', because then if the people are still buying Ivy Infotech's laptops then these laptops must have the fastest processors, else people would be buying some other company's laptops.

Weakener – So now that we have identified the conclusion, the evidence, and the assumption, the option that best tells us that the assumption may NOT be true has to weaken the argument. In essence, this option will provide us with some other reason (other than faster processors) why the sales of Ivy Infotech's laptops have been very high. (E) does this best and should be the correct answer.

For clarity, let's also take a look at the other options:

A. This was last year while the increase in sales has been this year. It is very much possible that because of this criticism Ivy Infotech equipped its laptops with faster processors. So by no stretch does this option weaken the argument.

B. Desktops and tablets are outside the scope of the argument. The fact remains that Ivy Infotech's laptops have outsold those of its rivals by a large margin. We need to show that this was not because of the faster processors and this option fails to do so.

C. This option states that overall Ivy Infotech has performed worse this year than it did last year but we are not concerned with this. The fact remains that Ivy Infotech's laptops have outsold those of its rivals by a large margin. We need to show that this was not because of the faster processors and this option fails to do so.

D. Looks good but doesn't necessarily weaken the argument. All the companies in Ireland source their processors from the same company does not mean that the processors are all the same. Those sourced by Ivy Infotech could very well be faster than those sourced by its rival firms.

E. This option gives you an alternative reason why Ivy Infotech has sold more laptops than its rivals. It was not because of demand side issue but because of supply side constraints. Because of the production bottlenecks at its rival companies' plants, Ivy Infotech's laptops were probably available in the market in much larger numbers than those of its rivals, which is why they sold more. Hence this option weakens the argument by providing you with an alternative explanation to the one mentioned in the stimulus.

Weakeners and Assumptions

Common sense dictates that the only way in which an option can weaken an argument is by raising doubts about the validity of its assumption. When you make an assumption, you immediately deny the possibility of any other scenario being true. The weakener will provide you with these alternate scenarios and hence raise doubts in your mind as to which explanation is the correct one.

Remember that an option will never weaken the argument by questioning its evidence or by trying to negate its evidence. The evidence is a fact so it can never be questioned. What can be questioned however is the conclusion that is arrived at by using this evidence. You can't question facts but you can always question an opinion.

So the answer to a weaken question will usually be the option that provides you with alternatives to what has been assumed in the argument.

Always weaken the connection between the Evidence and the Conclusion

Just like strengthen questions, on weaken questions also you must, at all times, try to weaken the connection between the evidence and the conclusion. Never weaken the conclusion in isolation (even if the argument asks you to weaken the conclusion).

According to a recent survey conducted in Unitown City, people who drove SUV's were much more likely to flout traffic rules than people who drove regular sedans. Hence, if the government wishes to reduce the incidence of road accidents, it should ban the sale of SUVs in the city.

Which of the following two options most weakens the argument?

1. The road condition in Unitown City is very poor, and it is much easier to drive SUVs on these roads than regular sedans.

2. The survey size comprised 5% of the population of Unitown City.

The conclusion of this argument is based on the evidence of the recent survey. The only way to weaken this argument is by questioning the integrity of this survey. Notice that you cannot state that the survey was never conducted, you can only question its integrity.

Option two states that the survey only comprised a very small population of Unitown City so it may not be representative of the entire population of Unitown City. For example, it is possible that people drive rashly in the neighbourhood where this survey was conducted, but the people in the rest of the city are safe drivers. Thus, option two definitely weakens the argument.

As against this, option one provides you with a reason why people should be allowed to drive SUVs. But if driving SUVs is going to lead to more accidents, then this may not be a good enough reason not to ban the sale of SUVs in the city. Hence this option is outside the scope of the argument.

So the takeaway is that you always try to weaken the link between the evidence and the conclusion. The evidence is there for a purpose and you must make use of it.

How to Approach Weaken Questions

1. Read the argument and be clear on the evidence and the conclusion

2. Try to predict the assumption because the weakener will, in some way, try to convince you that this assumption may not be valid

3. Go through the options and eliminate those that strengthen the argument or are otherwise outside the scope of the argument

4. Remember to take into consideration the evidence as well; don't just weaken the conclusion in isolation

Flaw

Questions

Flaw Questions

Flaw questions will ask you to identify a flaw in the author's reasoning. Keep in mind that all arguments have the same fundamental flaw – that they rely on one or more unstated assumptions. So in a flaw question you basically need to question the assumption made by the author.

> Ronald scored 600 on the GMAT while Derek scored 338 on the GRE. So Ronald performed much better than Derek did.
>
> Which of the following is the most serious flaw in the argument?
>
> (A) The argument does not take into account the possibility that Ronald's score could be a fluke
>
> (B) The argument does not take into account the past academic records of Ronald and Derek
>
> (C) The argument arrives at an extreme conclusion on the basis of unverified data
>
> (D) The argument assumes that standardised test scores are the best predictor of future success of an individual
>
> (E) The argument discounts the possibility that the GRE and the GMAT may have different scoring scales

Since this is a flaw question, you know that the stimulus will be worded in the form of an argument. So the first step is to identify the conclusion and the evidence of this argument.

Conclusion (What is the argument stating) – Ronald has performed better than Derek.

Evidence (Why is the argument stating this) – Ronald scored 600 on the GMAT and Derek scored 338 on the GRE, and since 600 is more than 338, Ronald must have performed better.

But does this make sense? Those of you who are aware of the GRE scoring pattern would obviously know that a 338 (out of 340) on the GRE is a much better score than a 600 (out of 800) on the GMAT. However the argument does not assume that you will know this or need you to know this.

For all you know the GRE could be scored out of 1000 and the GMAT could be scored out of 2000. The important thing is to notice that the argument does not mention this fact, which will then take you to the assumption.

Assumption (the unstated evidence) – The assumption now is fairly easy to predict – that the GRE and the GMAT are scored on the same scoring scale. Only if this is assumed can the argument conclude what it is concluding; if you negate this fact then the argument will fall apart.

Flaw – The flaw will always question the assumption. It will raise doubts in your mind as to what if the assumption was not true. Out of the five options in the above argument, (E) does this best and hence is the correct answer. The argument does not take into account the possibility that the GRE and the GMAT may have different scoring scales and that a 338 on the GRE may actually be a better score than a 600 on the GMAT.

For clarity, let's also take a look at the other options:

A. It really doesn't matter how Ronald arrived at that particular score as long as there a possibility that this score could still be worse than Derek's score

B. Past academic records are irrelevant because the argument is only concluding for the current tests taken by Ronald and Derek. The argument does not make a conclusion that Ronald in general is a better student than Derek.

C. There is nothing in the argument to suggest that the data is unverified.

D. The argument does not make any conclusions about how successful will the two candidates be in future.

E. The correct answer.

Flaw and Assumptions

As we have seen, the answer to a flaw question will always be linked to the assumption of the argument. In essence, the flaw is the fact that the argument is relying on an assumption in the first place. So a flaw will simply end up questioning the assumption at all times.

The wording of the Flaw Question stem

A flaw question will either directly ask you to identify the flaw in the argument or it could also make use of terms such as *vulnerable to the objection* or *vulnerable to the criticism*. Here are some common ways of wording flaw questions:

- The argument is flawed primarily because
- Which of the following most strongly indicates that the logic of the above argument is flawed?
- The argument is most vulnerable to which of the following criticisms/objections?

How are Flaw Questions different from Weaken Questions

So are flaw questions the same as weaken questions? The answer is that the two are similar but not the same.

There is one big difference between the two – a flaw is always from within the argument; it is simply the assumption stated in some other words and will never mention additional evidence. As against this a weakener will almost always mention additional evidence that can question the validity of the argument's assumption. You can only weaken an argument by bringing in an additional point whereas the flaw will always be inherent in the argument.

Because of this fact an option that mentions a flaw will always be worded in the form of a question or a doubt whereas an option that mentions a weakener will always be worded in the form of a fact or evidence.

For example, in the Ronald vs. Derek argument, the following can be a possible weakener:

- The GRE is scored out of 340 whereas the GMAT is scored out of 800

Now do you notice how this option is different from the one that mentioned the flaw? The flaw was just raising a doubt that the two scoring scales may be different whereas this option provides a fact that confirms that the two scoring scales are different.

Typical Flaws present in Arguments

There are some typical flaws that the GMAT likes to test students on. Let's take a look at some of them:

i. **Mistaking Correlation for Causation** – In such cases, the argument will state that X and Y take place together or one after the other, so X is the cause of Y i.e. what appeared to be a simple correlation is actually a cause and effect relation.

> The days on which Kevin wears a black shirt, he performs much better in his practice tests than he does on days on which he wears a shirt of some other colour. So on the day of the final test, Kevin must ensure that he wears a black shirt.

ii. **Confusing you with Absolute numbers and Percentages** – In such arguments, the author will try to confuse you by providing absolute numbers as evidence and concluding for a percentage or vice versa. You've already seen an example of this in the argument at the beginning of this chapter (Ronald vs. Derek). Here's another one:

> 10% of the total houses in London are for sale and 30% of the total houses in New York are for sale. So there are more houses for sale in New York than in London.

iii. **Representativeness** – In such arguments the author will assume a small sample size to be representative of a much larger population or group.

> The mayor of Rodham City does not seem to be very popular with the city's residents. Out of the 20 people that I spoke to this afternoon, as many as 15 said that they hated the mayor.

You'll see each of these argument types in much more detail later in this book when we discuss some typical argument patterns tested on the GMAT.

How to Approach Flaw Questions

1. Read the argument and be clear on the evidence and the conclusion

2. Try to predict the assumption because the flaw will always question the assumption in some manner

3. Look for some typical flaws based on the wording of the argument. If the argument mentions numbers, look for a correlation-causation problem; if it mentions a survey, look for a problem of representativeness, etc.

4. Remember not to confuse a flaw with an option that weakens the argument. If confused, go with the option that is directly connected to the argument's assumption

Inference

Questions

Inference Questions

Inference questions will ask you to infer or conclude something from the information given in the stimulus. The literal meaning of *infer* is to conclude something without it being explicitly mentioned. This is exactly what you are required to do on an Inference question – arrive at an option that is not explicitly stated in the stimulus but that can easily be concluded given the information in the stimulus. This presents its own unique problems that we will see later in this chapter.

First let's take a look at an example of an Inference question.

Last month three automobile manufacturers – Honda, Toyota, and Suzuki – launched new models of their respective sedans in Japan. The three models that were launched were similarly priced and had similar features. However the sales of Suzuki's new sedan have been far lower than those of Honda and Toyota's new sedans in the last one month.

The statements above best support which of the following as a conclusion?

(A) The people in Japan prefer cars manufactured by Toyota and Honda to those manufactured by Suzuki

(B) The people in Japan do not like cars manufactured by Suzuki

(C) Cars manufactured by Suzuki are notorious for their flimsy build quality and poor fuel efficiency

(D) In the last one month, Suzuki has earned less revenues from the sale of its new sedan than have Honda and Toyota

(E) Suzuki manufactures its cars primarily for the export market and not for domestic sale

Do remember that the stimulus of an Inference question may not necessarily be in the form of an argument. In fact, most often the stimulus will contain a set of facts like the one above. All that the above stimulus tells us is that Honda, Toyota, and Suzuki have each launched a new sedan last month and that the sales of Honda and Toyota's new sedans have been far greater than the sales of Suzuki's new sedan. These are all facts, and the author does not provide any conclusion on the basis of these facts.

Inference must be true and NOT may be true

One very important thing to keep in mind, while evaluating options on an Inference question, is that the correct option must be true under all conditions/possibilities. There may be some options which may be true under some situations and may not be true under others. These will not be the correct answer.

With this background, let's go through each of the options in the above question and see if we can arrive at the correct answer:

(A) This seems very obvious but such inferences must be avoided. For all you know Japanese people might actually prefer Suzuki cars the most but due to some supply constraints Suzuki's new sedan may not be available in the market.

(B) The earlier explanation applies to this option as well. In fact this option goes a step further by concluding that Japanese people do not like Suzuki cars at all. Since this may or may not be the case, this cannot be the correct answer.

(C) This looks very logical because it provides a very convincing reason why the sales of Suzuki's cars have been so low. But is that what we are supposed to do? Absolutely not. So this option does not even come close to being an Inference. It merely explains why the sales of Suzuki's new sedan may have been low but that is not what we are required to do in the argument.

(D) The Correct answer. The argument tells us that the three new sedans are similarly priced. Then if Suzuki has sold fewer cars (and by a large margin) than have Honda and Toyota, its revenues from the sale of this new sedan have to be lower than those of Honda and Toyota. This option must be true in all cases and hence has to be the correct answer.

(E) Like option C, this option again provides a logical explanation for Suzuki's low sales in Japan but this may or may not be the case. In any case we are not required to provide an explanation in the first place. So this cannot be a valid inference.

How will Inference Questions be worded?

In some cases an Inference question may directly ask you to infer something from the argument but in most cases it will be more confusingly worded and could be confused with some other confusion types.

i. Must be True Questions

You saw these questions earlier in the Assumption chapter; you can get questions with similar wording in Inference as well. Conceptually, the biggest difference between an Inference and an Assumption is the different places that they can be placed at in an argument. The following diagram will make it easier to grasp:

Assumption ⟶ **Argument** ⟶ **Inference**

So the assumption is what leads to the argument or what logically completes the argument. Without the assumption, the argument will be logically incomplete. The inference then follows from this argument. So Assumption comes before the argument and Inference comes after the argument. This conceptual difference leads to a slight difference in the manner in which these two *must be true* questions are worded:

Assumption: *Which of the following options must be true for the above argument to be true?*

Inference: *If the above argument/statements are true, then which of the following options must be true?*

Do you notice the difference between the two? An assumption question will look for an option that will make the argument true whereas an Inference question will start by assuming that the argument/stimulus is true and ask you to infer something from this.

ii. Questions with the word 'support'

The term *support* is used by two question types – Strengthen questions as well as Inference Questions.

Here is an example of each:

Strengthen: Which of the following options, if true, most strongly *supports* the hypothesis in the above argument?

Inference: The above hypothesis, if true, best *supports* which of the following as a conclusion?

The difference between the two will be the language of the question. A strengthen question will ask you to select an option *that supports* the argument whereas an Inference question will ask you to select an option *that can be supported* by the stimulus/argument i.e. that follows from the stimulus.

Tips for Inference Questions

— **Inference does not mean to summarize the argument** – An inference does not have to provide a logical conclusion to the stimulus nor does it have to be a summary of the argument. It just has to be a fact that can most definitely be concluded given the information in the stimulus. It goes without saying that there can be multiple inferences that can be arrived at from a given stimulus.

— **Don't bother predicting the answer** – Because multiple inferences can be made from a given stimulus, it doesn't make sense to predict the answer. Instead look at each option and try to eliminate extreme options or those that are outside the scope of the argument.

— **Always avoid Extreme options** – It is human nature to read too much between the lines. In fact this quality may even be beneficial or an asset in real life. However, on the GMAT this will prove to be a liability. If you read too much between the lines, you will most likely end up with extreme or strongly worded options, which will almost never be the correct answer to an Inference question. So avoid options that contain extreme words such as *must, always, only, cannot be determined, etc.* Instead go with options that contain vague words such as *usually, maybe, might, sometimes, possibly, etc.*

— **Never use outside knowledge to answer Inference Questions** – If you avoid extreme options, you will automatically end up avoiding making use of outside knowledge while evaluating options. For example, in the Suzuki argument, if you are aware that in real life Suzuki makes cars that are of a flimsy build quality or that are primarily meant for exports, then this may colour your judgement and make you select the wrong answer choice.

— **Assumptions play no role in Inference questions** – Unlike the five question types we saw earlier, Inference questions will not require you to identify the assumption in the argument. In most cases the stimulus won't contain an argument in the first place but just a set of facts.

— **Inference questions will also be tested on Reading Comprehension** – Yes, Inference questions will form a very important chunk of RC questions. As our recent Pareto analysis of the OG 13 revealed *(the Pareto Analysis is available for free download on the Free Resources section of our website),* almost half the RC questions in the OG 13 are Inference questions. These have been discussed in more detail in our RC Grail book.

— **Avoid Explain Answers** – A common wrong answer trap in Inference questions is an option that explains the situation in the stimulus. These options will look extremely logical to you but remember that the question is not asking you to explain the stimulus but to infer something from it.

How to approach Inference Questions

1. First read the stimulus. If it does not contain an argument or a discrepancy, then it will most likely be an Inference question

2. Read the question stem to confirm that you are indeed looking at an Inference question

3. Do not bother predicting the answer; immediately jump to the options

4. Don't spend too much time on each option. Take a quick look at all five options (maybe spending 10 seconds on each) and eliminate ones that are outside the scope of the argument.

5. By now you should've ideally narrowed down your choice to two or three options. Go through these options again and eliminate the ones that are extreme or very strongly worded

6. Sometimes Step 5 can directly lead you to the answer itself. In case you have more than one possibility for the correct answer, read the stimulus once again and try to identify the option that *must* be true based on this stimulus.

Explain

Questions

Explain Questions

Explain questions will ask you to provide the most logical explanation for the situation described in the stimulus. This stimulus will usually contain a contradiction or an anomaly i.e. a contrary to fact situation. Also the stimulus will always contain facts and won't be in the form of an argument.

Leading book publishers had predicted that the rampant illegal sharing of books online would have a detrimental impact on the sales of their physical books. However, the more illegal online sharing sites increase in popularity, the more physical books are being sold.

Which of the following options best explains why the sales of physical books have been increasing with the increase in online piracy?

A. The illegal sharing of books online has not become as popular as was expected

B. People in general find it more difficult to read books on a computer screen than reading a physical book

C. Book publishers have, in the last few years, invested heavily in advertising their books

D. A lot of people have discovered new authors through online book sharing sites and subsequently bought other books written by these authors because it is easier to read a physical book

E. The government has introduced heavy fines for those downloading books from online sharing sites

An explain question will never contain an argument so don't waste your time looking for the conclusion, evidence, and assumption. Instead try to quickly paraphrase the contradiction in the stimulus – it was expected that people will stop buying physical books because they could now download books for free from illegal online book sharing sites. However, as the free illegal book sharing sites gain popularity, the sales of physical books has also been growing similarly.

The correct option needs to explain why this has been the case. So let's take a look at each option in the question above:

A. This option directly questions a fact mentioned in the stimulus, which is something that can never be done on any CR question. The arguments states that illegal online book sharing is becoming more and more popular and we need to accept this fact as it is. We just need to show the connection between this fact and the fact that the sales of physical books have also been growing similarly.

B. This looks very good. However notice that it just provides you with a reason why people may not want to read books online. So in this case the sales of physical books should have remained unaffected or declined marginally. Then why have the sales been increasing? This option doesn't explain this fact. Remember that the correct answer has to explain both sets of facts and not just one of them.

C. This again addresses one part of the contradiction – why have the sales of books been increasing. But this option does not show the link between increase in illegal online sharing of books and the increase in sales of physical books.

D. The correct answer. This choice correctly identifies a link between the two sets of facts mentioned in the stimulus. People discover new authors through online book sharing sites, they like the book that they have read, and so they subsequently buy other books by these authors in the physical format because it is easier to read in this form.

E. Like B, in this case also the sales of physical books should have remained steady or changed slightly but what explains the increase in sales of physical books?

Based on the above analysis we can arrive at certain tips to keep in mind while attempting *Explain the Contradiction questions.*

Tips for Explain questions

— **Make sure you have identified the discrepancy in the argument before looking at the options** – A lot of times students rush to the options without realising what exactly they have to explain. As a result they go through all the five options and are not able to eliminate anything, so they go back and again read the stimulus to understand the discrepancy. Then they once again go through all the options leading to wastage of precious time.

— **Never explain just one side of the stimulus** – As you saw in some of the options above, the correct answer has to explain both sides of the contradiction and not just one side.

— **Never deny the evidence** – This applies to all Critical Reasoning question types. Never try to negate or question the evidence or facts provided in the stimulus. Take this as true at all times

— **The answer will always be from the outside** – The answer to an explain question will always be a new point that somehow explains the contradiction in the stimulus, so don't eliminate an option just because it contains terms that have not been mentioned in the stimulus. As long as it explains the discrepancy, it could very well be the correct answer

Common wrong answer choices on Explain questions

- Options that explain only one side of the contradiction
- Options that negate or question the validity of the facts/evidence provided in the stimulus

How to approach an Explain Question

1. Read the stimulus. If it contains an argument then it most likely will not be an explain question. However if it contains a discrepancy/contradiction/anomaly, then it has to be an *Explain* question
2. Read the question stem to confirm that you are indeed looking at an *Explain* question
3. Don't bother making a prediction because there are several possibilities that can explain the situation. Quickly scan through the options eliminating the common wrong answer types discussed above
4. By this time you should have come down to two choices, if not arrived at the correct answer. If confused go back and read the stimulus to understand the stimulus better. Restate the contradiction or discrepancy in your own words and check which option is best explaining both sides of it. Select this option and move on.

Logical Conclusion Questions

Logical Conclusion Questions

These questions are easy to identify because they always have a blank at the end. The question stem in effect asks you to fill in this blank in the most logical manner.

Some people think of a Logical Conclusion Question as an Assumption question while some think of it as an Inference question. However, we think these questions can also test you on other concepts (in fact most of these questions will come closest to the Strengthen question type) apart from the two mentioned, which is why we have decided to treat these questions as a separate question type. Also the OG 13 contains a lot of these questions which is why we have dedicated an entire chapter to this question type.

Let's take a look at an example

> Which of the following most logically completes the argument below?
>
> According to the policies of the prestigious City Golf Club, a one-time donation of five million dollars to the club's corpus guarantees an individual a lifetime membership to the club. However, more than fifty percent of the people who have become members of the Club after the adoption of this policy have become members without paying this amount. This fact, however, should not lead one to conclude that the Board of the Club is taking in members through unethical or underhand methods, since __________________.
>
> (A) all the Board members of the City Golf Club are highly respected citizens of the city
>
> (B) other prestigious clubs in the country also follow a similar policy for admitting members
>
> (C) the Club awards complementary memberships to a select few people who have done exemplary social work in that year
>
> (D) there are several other ways of obtaining the membership of the club as well
>
> (E) most people who apply for membership to the club have strong political connections

The stimulus of a Logical Conclusion Question will almost always be in the form of an argument. However identifying the conclusion, evidence, and assumption in these arguments may not be as straightforward as it is on strengthen or weaken questions. To understand this better, let's try to break up the above argument into its components.

The Evidence – According to the policies of the City Golf Club, anyone who pays a donation of five million dollars can get a confirmed membership to the club. However most of the people who have become members of the club after the adoption of this policy have not had to pay this amount.

The Conclusion – This is where things get interesting because this argument actually has two conclusions. One is an intermediate conclusion and one is the final conclusion which raises an objection to the intermediate conclusion.

Intermediate Conclusion –This conclusion states that the Board of the Club is taking in members through unethical means. This conclusion is the one arrived at on the basis of the above evidence and is made by a hypothetical person. Notice that this is not directly stated in the argument but is clearly implied by it.

Final Conclusion – This is the author's conclusion wherein he questions the intermediate conclusion or states that the intermediate conclusion is incorrect.

So all we need to do in the blank is to provide a reason that strengthens or supports this final conclusion of the author (or that weakens the intermediate conclusion made by the hypothetical person).

The Assumption – This is tricky, don't go looking for an assumption using the final conclusion of the argument. Remember you need to question the intermediate conclusion (and in any case it is this conclusion that was arrived at on the basis of the evidence and not the final one) so you need to find an assumption made in arriving at the intermediate conclusion.

The stimulus does not say that the *only* way to become a member of the club is by paying a donation of five million dollars. There could be several other ways of becoming a member as well. In arriving at the intermediate conclusion, the hypothetical person is assuming that the only way to become a member of the Club is by paying the donation of five million dollars.

To weaken the hypothetical person's conclusion (and to strengthen the author's conclusion) we just need to show that the above assumption is not true. Option (D) does this best and should be the correct answer.

Do not get confused as to whether you should look for the assumption in the intermediate conclusion or the final conclusion. A simple rule of thumb is to look for the conclusion between the evidence and the assumption. In the above argument the author does not provide any evidence for his final conclusion; in fact you have to provide this evidence in the blank. The evidence that is mentioned in the argument can only lead you till the intermediate conclusion so it is here that you must look for an assumption.

Let's also look at the other options for the sake of clarity:

(A) even if the Board members are highly respected citizens of the city, it is still possible that one of them could be indulging in some underhand dealings with prospective members

(B) For all you know the other clubs could also be following similar underhand practices.

(C) This only accounts for a few members but the stimulus clearly tells us that more than 50% of the members got in without paying the money, so how did these people get in?

(D) The correct answer

(E) So if these people indeed used their political connections to get their memberships than that is the same as resorting to unethical practices. So, if anything, this option could strengthen the intermediate conclusion and not weaken it.

Did you notice that the previous question was almost the same as a strengthen question. All you had to do was strengthen the author's final conclusion. So will all Logical Conclusion questions require you to strengthen the author's conclusion? Not necessarily.

So then how do you make out when you need to strengthen and when you need to do something else?

The answer is by looking at the word that leads to the blank. This is the word that comes immediately before the blank. If the word is *since* or *because* (like in the above argument) then you will definitely be required to strengthen the author's argument. Also the author's conclusion will be in the sentence that leads up to this word.

If the leading word/phrase is *that* or *it should be expected that,* then you will be required to make an inference from the information provided in the stimulus. In these questions remember to avoid extreme options and go with vaguely worded ones.

If the leading word is *assuming that,* then obviously you need to point out the assumption in the argument and the conclusion will again be the last sentence that leads up to the blank.

If the OG13 is anything to go by, most Logical Conclusion questions will have a *since* or *because* at the end and hence will require you to strengthen the argument.

How to Approach Logical Conclusion Questions

1. You'll easily be able to identify this question type by noticing the blank at the end of the stimulus. Quickly read the stimulus to get an idea of what the argument is talking about

2. Read the leading word into the blank to understand what exactly you are required to do. If you need to strengthen the argument or find the assumption in the argument, then quickly read the last sentence of the argument to understand what exactly is the final conclusion of the argument

3. Check if the argument contains any intermediate conclusion. If you find these difficult to spot, just try to paraphrase what conclusion is the evidence taking you to; is it the final conclusion of the argument or some other intermediate conclusion

4. Eliminate options until you are left with the correct one

Miscellaneous Questions

Bold Faced Questions

In bold faced questions, two complete sentences or parts of sentences are highlighted in bold. The question will usually ask you to identify the role being played by the two bold or highlighted parts in the overall context of the argument.

The difficulty with bold faced questions is that while you have to read the entire stimulus to understand what it is trying to state, you have to answer only for the bold part. A common trap the test maker uses is to give you options that describe the role played by the non-bold parts of the stimulus so as to trick you into going with these options.

The stimulus of a bold faced question will usually be in the form of an argument because only then can different sentences play different roles. In fact the stimulus will usually contain several arguments and counter arguments so as to make it difficult for you to grasp what exactly the parts in bold are doing.

Bold faced questions are generally regarded by test takers as one of the most (if not the most) difficult question types on the CR section. There are two reasons why these questions appear to be more difficult than the others:

1) You only have to answer for the bold parts

2) The confusing language of the options. All the options will use abstract language such as *the first is the opposition of the supposition assumed in the argument*

The options that you see on bold faced questions will always be worded in the form of *the first is doing x and the second is doing y*, further highlighting the fact that you only have to answer for the bold parts.

There is not one good reason for granting men paternity leave from work, while there are several good reasons to deny. For one, it would be an additional expense to businesses. Businesses are already facing tough times all over the world, so adding additional overhead is not an option. If the father acts like a father, he and the child will bond. **If the father doesn't act like a father, he and the child will not bond, regardless of whether he is at home or at work.**

In the argument given, the two portions in boldface play which of the following roles?

(A) The first is the primary conclusion of the argument and the second is a secondary conclusion

(B) The first is the advocacy of the argument and the second raises doubts about this advocacy

(C) The first provides evidence as to why a policy should not be adopted by businesses and the second further strengthens this evidence

(D) The first is a conclusion that the argument disagrees with; the second provides the reasoning behind this disagreement

(E) The first is the primary conclusion of the argument and the second provides reasoning supporting the primary conclusion

The argument provides reasons why men should not be granted paternity leave. The first bold part states the overall conclusion of the argument, and the second provides a reason in support of this conclusion. (E) states this best and is the correct answer.

Let's also look at the other options for more clarity:

A. While the first is indeed the primary conclusion of the argument, the second is not a secondary conclusion. In fact the second supports the primary conclusion of the argument by providing a reason why paternity leave is not required

B. While the first can be considered an advocacy, the second does not by any stretch raise doubts about this advocacy

C. The first bold part does not provide any evidence, it just provides the conclusion. The evidence is in the rest of the argument

D. The argument in fact agrees with the first bold part

E. The correct answer as described in option (A)

List of Common roles played by the bold parts

- **Final Conclusion** – This is the point that argument is trying to make
- **Intermediate Conclusion** – This often contrasts with the final conclusion
- **Counterpoint** – This is a statement that opposes something stated earlier in the argument
- **Background information** – This provides some context for the issue described in the argument

- **Prediction** – This will always be an opinion and talk about something happening in the future

- **Objection** – Questions or doubts something stated in the argument

On bold faced questions, once you've read the stimulus and before you look at the options, make a rough assessment of what exactly is the connection between the two parts of the argument in bold. This need not be a very precise relation, even something on the lines of *the first and the second are saying opposite things* or *the first is an evidence or a cause and the second is the conclusion or the effect* will do as this will help you eliminate incorrect options.

Remember that on bold faced questions you may not always be able to select the answer; rather you will often end up eliminating wrong answer choices to arrive at the correct answer. For example you could be stuck between two options both of which may look fine to you. Then you'll have to get down to reading every individual word in the shortlisted options and try to eliminate the incorrect ones.

For example if you know that the argument is neutral (i.e. it does not take any sides) and one of the options mentions the phrase *the author advocates* you immediately know that this cannot be the answer because the author is not advocating anything in the entire stimulus.

Approach to Bold faced questions

1. Read the stimulus and try to understand its overall meaning. The stimulus of bold faced questions usually tends to be long, so spend some time on this. As you read try to make out what role each sentence may be playing from the list of common roles that you saw earlier in this chapter

2. Once you've read the entire argument go back and just read the bold parts and try to identify the relation between them.

3. Quickly scan through all the options eliminating ones which are clearly incorrect. For example, if you have identified that the first bold part is an evidence, any option that states that the first bold part is a conclusion can immediately be eliminated.

4. Once you've narrowed down your choices to two or three, go through every word of the options and try to spot something that contradicts what is stated in the argument

Myth associated with Bold faced Questions

If I get a bold faced question on my GMAT, I must be doing well on the test – This is a common myth held by a lot of students but that's exactly what it is – a myth. We know of several students who got verbal scores in the 40s and yet did not get a single bold faced question. Similarly we also know of several students who got bold faced questions yet ended up scoring in the 20s. Another thing to keep in mind is that even if you do get a bold faced question, it may be the case that this was actually an experimental question.

The bottom line is that these questions are very rare so don't spend too much time sweating over these.

Main Point Questions

Main point questions ask you to identify the conclusion of the argument. The stimulus will always be in the form of an argument because the idea is to be able to arrive at a conclusion for the same. While conceptually these questions appear relatively simple (after all how difficult can it be to identify the conclusion of an argument?), the question is not actually just asking you to restate the conclusion.

In fact you will be required to sort of paraphrase the argument. So your answer will also have parts of evidence mentioned in it.

> The usual meaning of "free" is "devoid of cost or obligation". However, retailers often use the word for something which is merely included in the overall price. One common example is a "buy one, get one free" sale. The second item is not "free" under the normal definition, since, to obtain it, the buyer is obliged to pay the full cost of the first item.
>
> What is the main point of the argument?
>
> (A) Retailers often deceive buyers by creating the illusion of a discount; the buyer in fact does not get any discount
>
> (B) Whenever a retailer advertises an item as 'Free', the item is in fact not free
>
> (C) Retailers often trick customers by increasing the price of a product and then offering huge discounts on this increased price
>
> (D) An item cannot be free if one has to pay money in any form to acquire that item
>
> (E) The definition of 'FREE' can have different connotations for different people or groups of people

The main point of the argument is that an item cannot be called free if one has to pay a price (in the form of purchasing another item) to get the item in question. (D) states this best and is the correct answer.

Let's take a look at the other options for clarity:

> (A) There is no deception as the buyer does get a discount. He does not get the product completely free though because he has to buy another product to get the one that is free. But he still gets these at a lower price than he would otherwise have

(B) Extreme option. There could be some instances in which the item is free

(C) The argument never states this fact

(D) The correct answer

(E) Incorrect, according to the argument, the definition of 'Free' should only have one connotation

The best way of making Main Point questions difficult is to give you very close or ambiguous options so as to confuse you. If the answer choices are very far apart you can easily eliminate four incorrect ones; however, when the choices are extremely close, things could get a little tricky for you.

It always helps if you can paraphrase the entire argument in your own words before looking at the options. This will keep you from getting confused between two close choices.

A few years back the GMAT used to test students a lot on Main Point questions but of late these questions hardly appear on the test. Even the OG 13 contains barely 1 or 2 such questions.

Avoid answers

- Which only summarise a part of the argument
- Which restate a fact from the argument

Parallel Reasoning Questions

Parallel reasoning questions require you to understand the overall structure of the argument and to select an option that most closely matches this structure. These questions hardly appear any more on the GMAT. Because of the unusual requirement of this question, the options that you see on Parallel Reasoning questions will always be from fields other than the one that is mentioned in the argument. For example, the argument could talk about football and the correct answer could talk about medicines and diseases.

A lot of the times the argument could actually contain a flaw and the question stem could ask you to identify a similar flaw in the options given. The options in such cases will again be in the form of mini-arguments.

What you need to watch out for are options that are half right and half wrong, so make sure you read every word of the options carefully.

It is important to note that the correct option does not have to be in the exact same form as the original stimulus. For example, if the stimulus states the conclusion at the end, it is not necessary that the correct answer also states the conclusion at the end. The conclusion can very well be in the beginning as well. It is the overall reasoning that has to match and not the layout of the stimulus. This is why paraphrasing the argument will be very useful on Parallel Reasoning questions.

All the companies in Balco City have decided to freeze salary increments this year owing to the tough economic situation. Kevin works for a company in Balco city. So Kevin will face a salary cut this year.

Which of the following arguments exhibits flawed reasoning most similar to the one exhibited in the above argument?

(A) Jerry has not been keeping well of late because of which he hasn't been able to study at all. Therefore Jerry will perform poorly in the upcoming college examination

(B) Because of excessive traffic on the roads, Tom will not be able to arrive for a business meeting ahead of the scheduled time. So Tom might arrive late for the meeting.

(C) The temperature in the city may fall. Due to heavy rainfall, the temperature is not expected to rise.

(D) Tom likes to travel to his office by bus. Today there is a bus strike in the city, so Tom will not go to his office.

(E) Mobile phones will cost more in the next few months because the prices of mobile phones are not expected to be cut in the near future.

The stimulus for a Parallel Reasoning question will usually be in the form of an argument. So let's start by breaking up the argument into its components:

The Conclusion – Kevin will face a salary cut this year

The Evidence – Companies in the city in which Kevin works have decided not to provide salary raises this year

The Assumption – This is classic example of the fallacy which states that there are only two extreme possibilities for every event i.e. if an event does not happen then its opposite will take place. But there can always be a third possibility that nothing i.e. no change happens. For example, in the above argument if the salaries will not rise, then one can't conclude that they will necessarily fall. They might remain at the same level.

So the assumption in the argument is that if salaries don't increase then they will necessarily fall. To state it in more general terms, the assumption is that if X doesn't happen then the opposite of X will happen.

Let's try locating a similar flawed assumption in each of the options that are given to us:

(A) This is actually a very sound argument. If Jerry has not studied, he will most likely perform poorly in the upcoming college examination. So there is no flaw in this argument.

(B) This option looks good because if Tom can't reach before time, he does not necessarily have to reach late. He could also reach on time. However the problem is the use of the word 'might' suggesting that this may or may not happen. The correct option will conclude that this will definitely happen.

(C) This option puts the conclusion before the evidence. It is in effect saying that since the temperature is not expected to rise, it may fall. The problem again is, like option B, the use of *may*. We require a stronger word such as must to parallel the conclusion of the original stimulus.

(D) The original argument assumes that if X does not happen then the opposite of X will happen whereas this option assumes that if X does not happen, then Y will also not happen. Sometimes it may help to visualise arguments in terms of X and Y

(E) The correct answer. This option again puts the conclusion at the beginning and states that since the prices of mobile phones are not expected to fall in the near future, the prices will go up instead. This is exactly the kind of flawed reasoning we are looking for. The use of the strong 'will' makes this the correct answer.

SECTION 3

Common Argument Structures

In this chapter we will look at some typical argument structures that the GMAT uses. The questions will still be the same as we saw in the preceding chapters; nobody will ask you to identify the structure of the argument. It's just that if you spot the structure of the argument, it'll become very easy for you to arrive at the correct answer because you will know what exactly you are looking for even before you look at the options. You've already seen some of these in the Flaw chapter; now we'll take a more in-depth look at them.

Cause and Effect Arguments

These arguments basically state that just because two things happen together or one after the other, one is the cause of the other. Let's take a look at a very simplified example,

Jason is very intelligent because he studied at Harvard.

Cause – The fact that Jason has studied at Harvard

Effect – Jason becoming intelligent

If you look at this argument in terms of facts and opinion, the facts are that Jason is intelligent and that he has studied at Harvard. However the opinion is the connection between these two facts – that Jason is intelligent *because* he studied at Harvard.

Assumption – When the author concludes that the reason for Jason's intelligence is the fact that he studied at Harvard, he automatically assumes that nothing else could be responsible for Jason's intelligence except the fact that he studied at Harvard.

Cause and Effect Arguments and Weaken questions

On most occasions whenever you get cause and effect type of arguments, the question stem will require you to weaken the argument. There are two ways of weakening cause and effect type of arguments:

i) By providing another reason for the effect – As we saw above, in a cause and effect argument the author assumes that nothing else could be responsible for the effect in question. So if we can show that another cause could also lead to the same effect, then the argument is immediately weakened because we don't know what is leading to the effect for sure.

For example, the following can be a weakener for the Harvard argument above:

Both of Jason's parents are geniuses.

So then maybe Jason is very intelligent because of genetic reasons and not because he went to Harvard.

ii) By showing that the cause and effect could actually be upside down – This is a slightly more difficult to spot method of weakening cause and effect arguments. Even if two things happen together and we know that there definitely is a cause and effect relation between them, how do we know which of the two is causing the other; is X causing Y or is Y causing X. So if the argument concludes that X is causing Y, one way of weakening the argument is to show that it is actually Y that may be causing X.

For example

Because Jason was very intelligent, he got admitted into Harvard.

So it's is not that Jason became intelligent after going to Harvard but rather that he was intelligent which is why he could go to Harvard in the first place.

So if the argument in the stimulus is of the form A is causing B, then it can be weakened in the following two ways:

i) By showing that C can also lead to B

ii) By showing that it is not A that is causing B, but B that is causing A

Let's look at a proper example now.

A study has found that new ventures that are funded through bank loans are more likely to succeed than those funded by an entrepreneur's friends and relatives. The reason for this is not difficult to fathom. The obligation to pay a fixed instalment to the bank every month prevents the entrepreneur from getting complacent and increases his motivation to succeed.

Which of the following raises the strongest doubt on the above argument?

(A) Banks only fund those business ventures that have a very high probability of succeeding

(B) The study also showed the some ventures that had been funded by an entrepreneur's friends and relatives were extremely successful

(C) Most entrepreneurs agree that the pressure of repaying the bank loans acts as a positive stimulus for them

(D) It is an accepted fact that only those entrepreneurs opt for bank funding who are unable to generate funds from personal sources

(E) According to a different study, there is a strong correlation between an entrepreneur's educational background and the nature of his business venture

It's best to summarise cause and effect arguments in the form of a cause and an effect:

The Cause – Funding through bank loans

The Effect – A high probability of success for a new venture

As we saw there are two ways of weakening cause and effect arguments – either provide some other cause for the same effect or reverse the cause and the effect.

Option (A) reverses the cause and effect in the argument and is the correct answer. This option states that the cause was the business venture's high probability of success and the effect was funding provided by the bank. Had the bank felt that the venture may not succeed, it would not have funded the venture in the first place. So it is not because of the bank funding that the venture succeeded but because the venture was going to succeed that the banks funded it in the first place.

Let's look at the other options for clarity.

(A) The Correct Answer

(B) This doesn't tell you anything because of the use of the word *some*. Some ventures were successful and some were not. Had the option stated that *most* such ventures are very successful then it could have negated the argument (but this won't be the case because in that case the argument would be questioning the evidence itself, which can never be the case)

(C) This option actually strengthens the argument

(D) Under what conditions an entrepreneur opts for bank funding is irrelevant to the argument

(E) The nature of the entrepreneur's business venture is of no consequence to the argument.

Representativeness

Representativeness arguments will involve arriving at a generalized conclusion for a large population based on a sample or survey of a small sub set of the population.

For example,

> In response to a recent survey conducted by a newspaper in Quantos city, 70% of the respondents stated that they are very happy with the performance of the mayor and 20% stated that they are reasonably happy with the performance of the mayor. Only 10% of the respondents stated that they were unhappy with the mayor's performance. So, it seems safe to say that the residents of Quantos City are in general happy with the mayor's performance.

The Conclusion - The residents of Quantos City are in general happy with the mayor's performance.

The Evidence – The majority of respondents to a survey have expressed satisfaction with the mayor's performance.

The Assumption – The assumption is where the representativeness factor will come into play. What if this survey was conducted only amongst the economically well off residents? It is possible then that the poorer residents of Quantos City may actually be unhappy with the mayor's performance but their views haven't been taken into consideration at all in this survey.

So for the argument to hold true, the author of the argument has to assume that the survey mentioned in the argument is representative of the opinion of the entire population of Quantos city.

In general, whenever you see the terms *survey, poll, research, study, etc* mentioned in the evidence of any argument, immediately question whether this survey/poll/research is representative of the larger population as a whole. This will always be the assumption in the argument.

Then if you have to strengthen the argument, you will have to show that the survey/poll/research is indeed representative of the larger population whereas if you have to weaken the argument you will have to show that the survey/poll/research may not be representative of the larger population.

A strengthener for the above argument could be

> *The survey gave adequate importance to all demographic groups in Quantos City*

And a weakener could be

> *The survey comprised only 10% of the total population of Quantos City*

Notice that the strengthener and the weakener do not confirm or negate the argument. The strengthener simply removes one doubt from your mind and the weakener plants a doubt in your mind.

Number Arguments

Number Arguments are a mix of Maths and reasoning questions. These arguments will typically try to confuse you with their use of numbers.

For example

> Last year 300 undergrad students of Villa College managed to gain admission to the top ten graduate schools in the country. However, only 100 undergrad students of Havary College managed to gain admission to these schools. Thus, if you wish to study in the country's top ten graduate schools, your chances are higher if you pursue your undergrad degree from Villa College than from Havary College.

The Evidence – 300 undergrad students of Villa College gained admission into the country's top ten schools whereas only 100 undergrad students of Havary College gained admission to these schools

The Conclusion – A student's chances of gaining admission into one of the country's top ten graduate schools are higher if he attends Villa College than if he attends Havary College

On the face of it this argument looks very plausible. After all 300 is a much greater number than 100. However what if the total number of applicants at Villa College to the country's top ten graduate schools is 1000? Then the probability of a student getting into one of these top schools is 0.3 or 30%. And what if the total number of applicants at Havary College to the country's top ten graduate schools is 200? Then the probability of a student getting into one of these top schools is 0.5 or 50%.

So the chances of a Havary College student getting into a top graduate school are higher than those of a Villa College student. But this fact will make our argument fall apart. This leads us to the assumption in the argument.

The Assumption – The assumption has to be that the number of applicants to the country's top graduate schools from Villa College and Havary College is the same. Only then can 300 reflect a higher probability than 100.

So as you can see, number questions can be extremely confusing because the argument may appear completely logical to you at face value. It would help if you knew some common traps that the test maker uses to create number argument questions:

i. **A higher percentage could lead to a lower number and vice versa**

You can only make sense of percentages when you have a total number given to you. Looking at percentages in isolation can distort your perception of the data.

> For example, in Year 1 the total radio sales in country X were 100000 units and in Year 2 the total sales came down to 60000 units. In Year 1, 40 % of all radio sets sold were of Company A and in Year 2 this percentage increased to 60%

So you notice that even though Company A's share of the total radio sales increased from 40% to 60%, the total number of radio sets sold by Company A actually fell from 40000 in Year 1 to 36000 in Year 2.

ii. **A higher number could lead to a lower percentage and vice versa**

Again looking at absolute numbers, without taking into consideration the relevant percentages, can distort your perception of the data.

> For example, 10 students who study from Professor Roberts scored in the 90th percentile in their tests whereas 60 students who study from Professor Brown scored in the 90th percentile in the same test.

From the above data you may infer that Professor Brown is perhaps a better teacher than is Professor Roberts. However such an inference will be extremely erroneous because we don't know the total number of students taught by each of the Professors.

For example, if Professor Roberts taught only 20 students, then 50% of his students scored in the 90th percentile, and if Professor Brown taught 300 students, then only 20% of his students scored in the 90th percentile.

Tips for making Inferences from Number Arguments:

— For any number argument question you need three details – the total number, the absolute number and the percentage

— If the stimulus contains percentages, avoid answer choices that contain absolute numbers

— If the stimulus contains absolute numbers, avoid answer choices that contain percentages

Importance of Certain terms on GMAT Critical Reasoning

1. The use of some, many, most, and majority

While you may think that there is not much difference between these terms, there actually is a big difference. *Some* or *few* means more than one but *most* means more than 50%. This can have a huge bearing when you get down to eliminating incorrect options.

> Four out of five students who study from Professor Larry score above 75% in their exams. So the credit for their excellent performance must go to Professor Larry.
>
> Which of the following two options most strongly weakens the argument?
>
> 1. Some students who study from Professor Larry also take additional tuitions in the subject from Professor James
>
> 2. Most students who study from Professor Larry also take additional tuitions in the subject from Professor James

The argument is in the form of a cause and effect argument where the cause is Professor Larry and the effect is students getting excellent scores in their exams. The easiest way to weaken such arguments is to provide an alternative explanation (cause) for the effect.

Both the above options provide you with an alternative explanation – the fact that students also took classes from Professor James so maybe Professor James is the cause and not Professor Larry. So does this mean that both the options weaken the argument?

No it doesn't.

Option one states that *some* students who study from Professor Larry also take classes in the same subject from Professor James. However, this fact doesn't tell you anything relevant because some students maybe taking these extra classes and some may not. For example, say the total number of students who take classes from Professor Larry is 100 and 5 of them also take classes from Professor James.

Now the argument tells you that on an average 80 out of these 100 students (four out of five) score 75% or above in their exams. Then even if the 5 students who studied from Professor James scored well because of Professor James' teaching, how do you account for the remaining 75 students. It is still very probable that they performed well because of Professor Larry's teaching. So the use of *some* does not take you to the answer.

However *most* means more than 50% so out of the 100 students who study from Professor Larry, if 51 also take classes from Professor James , then it definitely raises a doubt as to whether these students are doing well because of Professor Larry or Professor James. Thus this option weakens the argument by providing an alternate explanation for the stated conclusion.

The takeaway is that words such as *some, many, and few* will rarely give you the answer; instead look out for words such as *most, majority, etc.*

However don't follow this strategy as a blind rule. There is a situation in which *some* can give you the answer. Say an argument concludes that nobody in America uses wood fired stoves anymore. Now if one of the options were to say that a *few or some* people in America still use these stoves, then this option would definitely weaken the argument.

2. The use of 'not' in the options

This will be relevant only for Assumption questions. As you saw earlier in the chapter on Assumptions, the use of *not* in one or more options is an indicator that you may be looking at a passive assumption. Let's take a look at the earlier argument once again:

> Four out of five students who study from Professor Larry score above 75% in their exams. So the credit for their excellent performance must go to Professor Larry.
>
> Which of the following is an assumption in the argument?
>
> 1. The fact that they study from Professor Larry is the only reason that his students do well in the exam
>
> 2. The fact that most of the students who take classes from Professor Larry also take classes from Professor James is **not** the reason why these students perform well in the exams

Option one is definitely assumed in the argument because there can be several other reasons why these students perform well in their exams – maybe they refer to several additional books, maybe they do more research on their own, etc. So for the argument to conclude that the cause of the students' good scores is Professor Larry, it has to assume that nothing else could be the cause of this.

How about option B? Interestingly, option B is also an assumption in the argument. This option logically follows from the earlier assumption. If the argument assumes that the only reason students do well is because they attend Professor Larry's classes, then it automatically also assumes that any other explanation for the said fact cannot be correct. Option B negates the possibility of one such explanation being true, so it is also an assumption in the argument.

Basically option A is an active assumption and option B is a passive assumption.

3. The use of EXCEPT in the Question stem

If we were to ask you what is the opposite of a strengthen option what will you say? Most likely 'weaken'. It is this thought process that you will have to guard against in EXCEPT questions. Technically, the opposite of a strengthen option will be an option that does not strengthen. The fact that this option does not strengthen does not necessarily imply that it will weaken the argument. It may just be an irrelevant fact, or it may be an inference, etc.

So, if the question stem tells you that *each of the given options strengthens the argument EXCEPT* then you need to identify four options that strengthen the argument and the remaining fifth option will be the answer – this option may or may not weaken the argument.

Hence, in EXCEPT questions, when you encounter an option that looks irrelevant don't eliminate it since this may be the correct answer; in fact this option will most likely be the correct answer.

SECTION 4

Critical Reasoning Practice Set

Aristotle Critical Reasoning Practice Set

1) Financial Expert: Our country has a very high debt-to-GDP ratio and it's difficult for a country with a high debt-to-GDP ratio to grow in a dynamic manner. Moreover our debt is growing higher and that means inflation is getting worse. All in all, our country is badly managed these days.

Which of the following assertions is most strongly supported by the passage?

(A) High debt has an adverse impact on the inflation rate

(B) It is not possible for a badly managed country to grow in a dynamic manner.

(C) High level of debt is extremely detrimental to the growth of a country

(D) Growing inflation is the sign of a badly managed country

(E) Whatever growth is happening in this particular country cannot possibly be dynamic growth

2) In the early 1960s, Myanmar was the richest country in Asia, but then it closed its economy to the outside world and is now the poorest country in the region. However, Myanmar is now opening up its economy to the outside world once again, and so will soon regain its former glory. Thus it makes sense for smart investors to invest in Myanmar.

Which of the following is an assumption on which the argument depends?

(A) A closed economy will rapidly deplete the financial resources of a country

(B) The countries that dealt with Myanmar in 1962 will still be interested in dealing with it

(C) If Myanmar does not open up its economy to the outside world, it will continue to remain poor.

(D) The severe internal unrest that has continued in Myanmar for the last several years is not responsible for its current financial state.

(E) At least some smart investors are currently aware of Myanmar's past glory

3) With less than 20 per cent market share, Cherico Airline has been steadily losing ground to other competing airlines. However, the recent addition of the Dreamliner aircraft to its fleet might just turn the tide for Cherico. The Dreamliner claims 15 per cent more fuel efficiency than competing similar aircrafts and cheaper maintenance costs. With the induction of these planes, Cherico will get a competitive advantage over its more aggressive rivals, which will be saddled with older aircrafts and get deliveries of their own Dreamliners only in 2014.

Which of the following would it be most useful to determine in order to evaluate the argument?

(A) Whether it is possible for Cherico to cut costs even more by reducing the number of stewards in the air plane

(B) Whether it is possible for Cherico to improve the Dreamliner's fuel efficiency even further by restricting the amount of luggage passengers can carry

(C) Whether Cherico can increase its revenues by charging for the meals it serves in its aircrafts

(D) Whether the Dreamliner's maintenance costs will be substantially lower than those of Cherico's rivals' aircrafts

(E) Whether it will be possible for Cherico's rivals to somehow get deliveries of their own Dreamliners expedited

4) G. Bell Corporation, a manufacturer of mobile handsets, has claimed to have become the leading seller of mobile handsets, in terms of units sold, in the country. According to latest figures released by all the handset manufacturers in the country, G. Bell Corporation managed to sell 80 per cent of the total handsets that it manufactured during the year whereas the market leader, H. Wells Corporation, managed to sell only 50 per cent of its total handsets.

Which of the following identifies a flaw in G. Bell Corporation's reasoning?

(A) It does not take into account H. Wells Corporation's huge book of advance orders for handsets that need to be shipped during the next year

(B) It incorrectly assumes that the current trend will continue into the next year as well

(C) It makes no comparison of the average price at which G. Bell Corporation sold its handsets with the average price at which H. Wells Corporation sold its handsets

(D) It does not take into account the total number of handsets sold by either manufacturer

(E) It does not take into account the total market size for mobile handsets in the country

5) The supply of iron ore, the most important component in steelmaking, has been steadily declining in Marco city. This has forced steel manufacturing units in Marco city to source iron ore from far off mines leading to an increase in their transportation costs. Because transportation costs make up a large chunk of the total cost of steelmaking, the steel manufacturers in Marco city have had no option but to increase the selling price of their steel. This has in turn led to an increase in the retail price of utensils and other articles of daily use made of steel. Since the retail consumers now have to pay more for these steel items, while their earnings remain unchanged, they have decided to cut down on their non essential expenditure such as that on movie tickets. This has led movie theatres in Marco city to reduce their ticket prices.

Which of the following provides the most support for the assertion that the prices of movie tickets in Marco city will continue to decline in future?

(A) The people of Marco city will not be willing to cut down their expenditure on eating out

(B) After the inauguration of the Goldport Bridge, expected to happen very soon, the transportation costs to Marco city will be halved

(C) There are no blockbuster movies with stellar star casts lined up for release anytime soon

(D) The supply of iron ore to Marco city is expected to go down even more in the near future

(E) Residents of Marco city view movie tickets as non essential items of expenditure

6) The Starbeans cafe has recently hired a new manager. The manager, within a few days of joining, made some drastic changes as a result of which the number of people visiting Starbeans everyday fell by almost 40%. However the revenue during this same period almost doubled.

Which of the following, if true, most helps to explain how the revenues of Starbeans increased despite the falling footfalls?

(A) The manager appointed a new coffee bean supplier who charges much lower rates than did the earlier supplier, resulting in substantial cost savings.

(B) The manager changed the interior of the cafe, making the seats much more comfortable than the earlier seats and adding more colour to the walls.

(C) The manager's monthly salary is directly linked to the revenue; the more the revenue the more salary he gets.

(D) The manager increased the average price of every item on the menu, in some cases even doubling the original price

(E) The manager fired some of the staff, thereby cutting down Starbean's salary cost by half.

7) According to a report by the American Staffing Federation (ASF), the government's new policy for the retail industry is likely to create 2 million jobs for fresh graduates over the next three years. The ASF has, thus, welcomed the government's move to implement this policy across the nation as its implementation will lead to a lowering of the national unemployment rate.

Which of the following, if true, would cast the most serious doubt on the accuracy of AFS' conclusion?

(A) Opponents of the policy will not allow the government to implement the policy anytime soon

(B) The new policy will result in a large number of uneducated workers becoming redundant and, as a result, losing their jobs

(C) There are several other ways of lowering the national unemployment rate available to the government

(D) The nation faces more serious problems than unemployment and the government should instead focus on resolving those first

(E) The implementation of the new policy is going to cost the government a considerable amount of money so the government will most likely increase corporate tax rates to recover this amount

8) It may soon be possible to insure your Facebook, Twitter, and other social media accounts against the nuisance of hacking as a company has launched the country's first social media insurance. The insurance includes the cost of disabling accounts, suppressing offensive material and stopping any legal action triggered by hacking, for example if a hacker posts illegal material under a victim's name.

Which of the following can properly be inferred from the statements above?

(A) Social media insurance will make it possible for individuals to sue hackers who post offensive content in their name

(B) The launch of social media insurance will, most likely, lead to a fall in the incidence of hacking on social media sites such as Facebook and Twitter

(C) There is a cost associated with enabling and disabling a social media account

(D) Under current laws it is possible for a person to be sued for posting offensive material online even if the person did not post the material himself

(E) Social media insurance will only be available for Facebook and Twitter users

9) According to those in favour of privatisation of Social Security in the US, the current system is impossible to sustain. Decades ago, there were many more workers for every recipient but now the situation has reversed. Sooner or later, the fund will not be able to meet its obligations, because there will be more payments going out, than income coming in. Privatizing the system for the future recipients, while gradually phasing out the system for current and near-term recipients, is probably the best way to keep the system viable.

The answer to which of the following questions would be most useful in determining whether privatisation of Social Security in the US would be a good idea?

(A) Whether privatization has proved successful for other government provided services such as employee provident funds

(B) Whether the population of the US is likely to increase significantly in the future

(C) Whether the growth in the number of workers is the US is likely to outstrip the growth in the number of dependents in the future

(D) Whether privatization of social security will lead to large scale protests by US citizens

(E) Whether taking loans can help the Social Security system tide over the problem of the reduction in funds coming in to the system

10) Large corporations use several strategies to minimize their tax payments, without doing anything explicitly illegal. One such strategy involves the use of transfer pricing, when subsidiaries in different countries charge each other for goods or services "sold" within the group. This is particularly popular among technology and drug companies that have lots of intellectual property, the value of which is especially subjective. These intra-company royalty transactions are supposed to be arm's-length, but are often priced to minimise profits in high-tax countries and maximise them in low-tax ones.

If the above statements are true, then which of the following could be a strategy adopted by a company that wants to get the maximum benefit out of transfer pricing?

(A) Sell its subsidiary located in a high tax rate country products at low prices

(B) Charge its subsidiary located in a low tax rate country higher prices for products sold

(C) Pay its subsidiary located in a high tax rate country high prices for products bought

(D) Pay its subsidiary located in a low tax rate country low prices for products bought

(E) Pay its subsidiary located in a low tax rate country high prices for products bought

11) Which of the following best completes the passage below?

When telecom companies, used to reporting several million new customers in a month, do the opposite and report a sharp fall in that number, you know that the country's most dynamic industry has entered a new, more troubled phase. However, this statistic may not necessarily be as much of a cause for concern as it looks because ________________________.

(A) mobile phone companies have huge cash reserves so they will not face the problem of cash flow for a few months at least

(B) inflated claims about new customer acquisition have been very much a part of the telecom industry story so far

(C) the sales of mobile phone handsets haven't fallen down appreciably

(D) other competitors have not entered the market in huge numbers

(E) mobile phone companies are making huge investments in widening their network coverage

12) The main purpose of business is to maximise shareholder value over the long term by selling goods or services. Thus, employees who use funds for anything other than to increase their sales are simply cheating the shareholders.

Which of the following is an assumption made in drawing the conclusion above?

(A) Most business owners would agree with the above definition of the purpose of a business

(B) Increasing sales is not the only way to maximise shareholder value

(C) Spending money on making the workplace more comfortable for employees will not lead to increased worker productivity and in turn increased business profits

(D) The only function of a business is to maximise returns for its shareholders

(E) According to this definition, many employees could be accused of cheating

13) The prime principle of economics is that prices are determined by supply and demand, not by costs. Some products may cost 90 cents and sell for dollar, while others go for a dollar yet cost only a cent to make. The second producer is neither a profiteer nor an exploiter, and the first producer is neither a benefactor nor a patron. Both producers merely respond to market signals based on supply and demand.

If the statements above are true, which of the following must be true?

(A) How much it costs to manufacture a product is not the primary determinant of its selling price

(B) A product with a low manufacturing cost is more likely to succeed than a product with a high manufacturing cost

(C) A manufacturer who sells a product with a low manufacturing cost at a high price to the customer is deceiving the customer

(D) If a product costs a lot to manufacture then its manufacturer must ensure that he does not sell the product at a high price

(E) A manufacturer who uses manufacturing costs of a product as a basis to determine the selling price of the product is bound to fail

14) A jewellery manufacturer produces rings in two metals – gold and platinum. The manufacturer has noted that, over the last three years, the gold rings have consistently outsold the platinum ones by a large margin, even though the designs available in both the metals are exactly the same. This has led the manufacturer to conclude that consumers prefer gold to platinum.

Which of the following, if true, most seriously weakens the argument?

(A) Over the last three years, diamond rings have outsold both gold and platinum ones

(B) Jewellery buyers give more importance to design than to the metal used

(C) Platinum is easier to maintain than is gold

(D) Platinum rings take longer to produce than do gold rings

(E) Gold rings cost considerably less than do platinum ones

15) The country has recently been shaken by the increase in incidents of corruption amongst the political class and the bureaucracy. The solution clearly is to appoint an independent investigating body headed by a person of repute who can investigate such cases of corruption and punish those found guilty.

The conclusion above would be more reasonably drawn if which of the following were inserted into the argument as an additional premise?

(A) The appointment of the independent body is the only way to combat corruption

(B) The independent agency will itself not fall prey to corruption

(C) Corruption is not present outside the political class and the bureaucracy

(D) The punishment meted out by the investigating agency will not act as deterrent for people/agencies susceptible to corruption

(E) If not controlled immediately, the problem of corruption can spiral out of control

16) Almost all arguments against the theory of evolution stem from the fact that it is very difficult to prove how a group of non living elements can combine together and give rise to life. However, just because something cannot be proved with certainty today doesn't mean that the possibility isn't there. Remember, there was a time when almost the whole world believed that the Earth was the centre of the universe until Galileo came by and proved otherwise.

The statements above, if true, best support which of the following assertions?

(A) At one point of time, Galileo was the only person who believed that the earth was not the centre of the universe

(B) A majority of scientists do not agree with the theory of evolution

(C) It is difficult to prove the theory of evolution with certainty

(D) When Galileo stated that the sun and not the earth was the centre of the universe, he was called insane by his compatriots

(E) Everything that at one time seems impossible will at some point in the future become possible

17) 30 years ago residents of Pandora County used to buy an average of 10 books every year. Today the residents of Pandora County buy an average of 3 books every year. Therefore it can be concluded that book sales in Pandora County must have fallen over these 30 years.

The argument above rests on which of the following assumptions?

(A) The residents of Pandora County used to have more free time 30 years ago than they do now

(B) The residents of Pandora County have many more activities that vie for their attention today than 30 years back

(C) The population of Pandora County hasn't increased significantly in the last 30 years

(D) The literacy rate hasn't significantly changed in Pandora County over the past 30 years

(E) Those residents of Pandora County who used to read 30 years ago have now not become too old to read

18) Which of the following most logically completes the argument below?

A new palm vein scanning technology is being developed by scientists that could be used with laptops or other tablet devices. This technology involves the use of a biometric sensor that can scan the unique pattern of veins in a person's palm to verify his identity. This technology could do away with the problem of remembering multiple passwords to access different websites. However the technology would require new biometric sensors to be built into computers but this should not be a hindrance in the success of the new technology, because____________________________.

(A) the new technology is bound to be extremely popular with computer users

(B) the biometric sensors do not cost a lot of money and are available in plentiful supply

(C) most people have forgotten one or more of their passwords at some point in their lives

(D) there is almost always a market for innovations such as these

(E) the biometric sensors can be easily and cost effectively built into computers

19) Switzerland's national rail company has accused Apple of stealing the iconic look of its station clocks for Apple's new operating system. According to the rail company, both designs have a round clock face with black indicators except for the second hand, which is red.

Which of the following, if true, most seriously weakens the argument above?

(A) Apple has never been accused of copying by any other person or organization in the past

(B) Apple is know the world over for its unique product designs

(C) The designer who created the watch design for Apple's operating system has never visited Switzerland or any other European country for that matter

(D) All round face clocks across the globe are created out of the same design philosophy

(E) The Switzerland National Rail Company has itself been accused in the past of copying the platform design of a neighbouring country's railway platform

20) Angel dusting is a process wherein an ingredient, which would be beneficial in a reasonable quantity, is instead added by manufacturers to their products in an insignificant quantity so that they can make the claim that their product contains that ingredient, and mislead the consumer into expecting that they will gain the benefit of that ingredient. For example, a cereal may claim it contains "10 essential vitamins and minerals", but the amounts of each may be only 1% or less of the Reference Daily Intake, providing virtually no benefit or nutrition.

If the above statements are true, which of the following could be an example of Angel dusting?

(A) A laptop that claims to have the longest battery backup, actually has a backup just 10% longer than is provided by its closest competitor

(B) A book that claims to cover all the concepts of Organic Chemistry actually provides just one example of each concept

(C) A vitamin capsule that claims to contain 23 vitamins and amino acids contains less than 3% of each

(D) A protein shake that claims to contain a magic ingredient that can make muscles grow faster, only contains 20% of this ingredient's daily recommended intake

(E) An apartment that claims to have used Italian marble for its flooring has used exactly one slab of Italian marble and the remaining ninety-nine slabs of regular marble.

21) In the year 2000 olive oils made up just 40% of the liquid oils market, with standard oils taking 52% and speciality oils accounting for the remainder. But now, fuelled by health concerns and a general move towards premium products, the tables have turned. Today, the olive oil sector is worth some $104 million and alone accounts for an estimated 51% of the total market.

Which of the following conclusions can most properly be drawn from the information above?

(A) In 2000, the total worth of the olive oil sector was less than $104 million

(B) The total sales of the standard oils at present time are lower than their sales in 2000

(C) Olive oil is healthier than all other liquid oils available in the market

(D) The market share of the standard oils category today must have declined from what it was in 2000

(E) The total worth of the specialty oil category today is higher than what it was in 2000

22) The Langova National park is a breeding ground for several migratory birds. The Spot-breasted Laughing Thrush, an extremely rare species of bird, has been sighted only in the Langova National park of late. The people who have sighted this bird in the park have claimed that it is possible to sight this bird only through the use of binoculars. Barry is visiting the Langova National Park next week and he will be carrying an extremely powerful pair of binoculars with him. Therefore it is safe to conclude that, as long as Barry has his binoculars on him, he will most definitely manage to sight the Spot-breasted Laughing Thrush.

Which of the following indicates a flaw in the reasoning above?

(A) It fails to take into account the possibility of sighting the Spot-breasted Laughing Thrush at places other than the Langova National Park

(B) It mistakes a necessary condition for a sufficient condition

(C) It is based on a series of assumptions, rather than on facts

(D) It does not take into account the possibility that Barry could lose or damage his binoculars on way to the park

(E) It does not take into account the possibility that Barry may sight some other equally rare species of bird

23) Jim Rogers: It's very difficult for foreigners to do business in India because India doesn't like foreigners and keeps them away. The biggest proof of this is Walmart, which has many stores in China, but not a single fully-owned store in India, simply because India doesn't like overseas businessmen.

Which of the following is an assumption made in drawing the conclusion above?

(A) There is nothing that can make India like foreign businessmen

(B) The fact that Walmart has many stores in China proves that China loves foreigners

(C) The limited size of the Indian market hasn't stopped Walmart from entering India

(D) Any foreign company other than Walmart is also not present in India

(E) China's policies are probably more favourable towards foreigners than are India's policies

24) Which of the following most logically completes the argument?

A recent experiment has revealed that a person stands the best chance of surviving a plane crash if he or she is sitting at the back of the aircraft. A Boeing 727 was crashed on purpose into the Sahara desert and various aspects of the impact were analysed. One of the findings of this experiment was that dummies placed at the back of the airplane suffered much less damage than the ones placed at the front. Thus, when travelling by airplanes, you would be much better off sitting at the back, assuming ____________________.

(A) that all the seats at the back of the plane haven't already been booked

(B) that the plane will be flying over the Sahara desert

(C) that the plane is manufactured by Boeing and has been part of the test described in the stimulus

(D) that the plane does not crash on its tail

(E) that these results apply to aeroplane crashes in general, and not just to those of old 727s into sand.

25) According to some people, income tax should be done away with in the US since there are several other ways to collect taxes. A few countries in Europe have successfully abolished income taxes by raising other taxes such as sales tax. Of course this makes products more expensive but with the added amount of money you would receive on your paycheck, you will still be better off than you were paying income taxes.

Which of the following, if true, provides the most support for the argument above?

(A) The prices of products in European countries, when converted into US dollars at current rates are very similar to their prices in the United States

(B) The increase in prices of products because of the increased sales tax rate will not more than offset the benefit of not paying any income taxes

(C) The legislative body in the United States has stated that it will support the move to abolish income tax

(D) Apart from increasing sales tax, the government can also increase other special taxes such as those on petroleum products

(E) The government has enough funds in reserve currently to be able to absorb any shock because of lowered tax collection

26) I do not agree that wage disparity still exists between men and women. Almost all salaried individuals today are paid based on their qualification and experience and not their sex. It is only the lower labour class where the disparity still exists, but this is justified because there are certain tasks requiring physical strength, such as carrying heavy construction material, that can only be done by men.

If the above statements are true, which of the following is an example of a wage disparity on the basis of gender?

(A) A company pays its management trainees, most of whom are females and have just passed out from business schools, a lower salary than it pays to its senior partners, most of whom are males

(B) A male labourer who does not do any physically taxing work is paid a lower wage than a male labourer who does physically taxing work

(C) A female employee at a managerial level in a company gets a lower salary than a female employee who has joined the company as a trainee but whose uncle is a partner in the company

(D) A male labourer who does not do any physical work is paid a higher wage than a female labourer who does not do any physical work

(E) A male manager working for Company X gets paid a higher salary than does a female manager with similar experience working for Company Z

27) A study of 1000 American citizens has found that 70 per cent of them would not work for a company with bad reputation even if they were unemployed and that nearly 90 per cent of them would consider leaving their current jobs if they were offered another role with a company that had an excellent corporate reputation. Of those willing to work for a company with a bad reputation, the research found that, on average, it would take doubling an employee's salary for them to make such a jump.

If the statements above are true, which of the following conclusions is most strongly supported by them?

(A) At least 10% of the people in the survey would not mind working for a company with a bad reputation but would also consider leaving their current jobs to join another company with excellent corporate reputation

(B) The survey is representative of the worker pool across the United States

(C) At least 25% of the people in the survey would agree to do an unethical act if their salary was substantially increased

(D) For US workers, higher salary takes precedence over the reputation of the company they work for

(E) If a company in the US expects to attract the best talent, it must either have an excellent corporate reputation or be ready to pay high salaries

28) One way in which companies can increase their productivity is by making use of telecommuting. Many office workers waste a lot of time in their cars or other modes of road transport every morning trying to reach office, and a lot of them spend their day attending video conferences and typing emails, activities which could easily be carried out from the comfort of their homes. So it makes sense for companies to encourage their employees to use telecommuting services and work from home rather than travel to the office every day

In order to evaluate the above argument, it would be useful to determine each of the following EXCEPT:

(A) Whether the cost of telecommuting will more than offset the increased productivity that comes about from its use

(B) Whether the day to day work of most companies involves physical interaction amongst their employees

(C) Whether a large part of the work of an average employee can be conducted using telecommuting services

(D) Whether the use of telecommuting service will lead to increased revenues for the companies adopting this service

(E) Whether the general traffic situation is likely to dramatically improve in the future

29) Barney has noticed a unique trend in his college test results over the last two semesters. When Barney was in Semester 1 he studied for two hours every day and got a score of 80 on 100 in his final test. In semester 2, Barney studied for four hours every day, yet he only scored 60 on 100 in his final test.

Which of the following, if true, most helps to explain why Barney's grades are declining even though he is spending more time studying every day?

(A) Barney studies with more concentration now than he used to in semester 1

(B) Even though his grades have gone down, Barney has become much more knowledgeable now than he used to be earlier

(C) Barney's classmates also, on an average, scored higher in semester 1 than they did in semester 2

(D) Barney participated in several sporting activities in the first semester

(E) In Barney's college, the topics taught in semester 2 are considerably more difficult than those taught in semester 1

30) Researchers have found that one in five patients hospitalized for heart attack experiences a major depression. According to the cardiologists who conducted the research, the depressed patients are fifty five percent more likely than other heart attack patients to need hospital care for a heart problem again within a year and three times as likely to die from a future attack or other heart-related conditions.

If the statements above are true, which of the following must be true?

(A) If a person dies of a heart attack, there is a high probability that he may have been suffering from depression as well

(B) If a patient needs to be re-hospitalised for a heart related problem within a year of his earlier heart attack, it is very likely that he may be suffering from depression

(C) There are some similarities between symptoms of depression and symptoms of a heart attack in a patient

(D) Depressed people are more likely to die of a heart attack than are people who do not suffer from depression

(E) Suffering from a heart attack can lead to depression in some people

31) The real estate market in Kayman city, which had so far been insulated from the weak demand for real estate in the rest of the country, is finally starting to feel the heat. According to a real estate advisory firm, the sales of residential property in Kayman city this year decreased by almost 25% from the same period last year.

Which of the following, if true, most strengthens the above argument?

(A) The sales of residential property in the rest of the country did not fall by more than 25% this year

(B) The sale of commercial property did not comprise the majority of real estate transactions in Kayman City this year

(C) A percentage decrease is the same as a decrease in the absolute number of sales of residential property in Kayman City this year

(D) The reduction in the sales of residential property in Kayman City is a recent phenomenon

(E) Most of the reduction in sales of residential property in Kayman City has come about because of the steep increase in interest rates charged by banks on home loans

32) A recent survey of buyers of luxury cars in Beecham city has revealed that males who are between 40 and 50 years of age and who live in the Southern part of the city are more likely to buy these cars than is any other demographic group in the city. Maxpages is a magazine that contains articles primarily relevant to males in the age group of 40 to 50 years and is circulated only in the Southern part of Beecham city. Using the findings of this survey, Terence, who owns two luxury car showrooms in Beecham city, has decided to advertise in the Maxpages magazine.

Which of the following would it be most useful to know in determining whether Terence should advertise in the Maxpages magazine?

(A) What is the exact number of luxury cars that were sold in all of Beecham city in the last one year?

(B) What percent of the total car market is the luxury car market in Beecham city?

(C) Do women and children play a major role in determining which luxury car to buy?

(D) Is the luxury car market in Beecham city expected to grow over the next few years?

(E) Will it would be cheaper to advertise in some other magazine that is targeted at people of all age groups?

33) Which of the following best completes the passage below?

A study was recently conducted to determine whether power lines caused some kind of negative health effects. The researchers surveyed everyone living within 200 meters of high-voltage power lines over a 15-year period and looked for statistically significant increases in rates of over 1000 ailments. The study found that the incidence of childhood leukaemia was four times higher among those who lived closest to the power lines. However, this statistic by itself should not be a cause for alarm, because__________________________.

(A) child leukaemia can also be cause by other genetic factors

(B) another study has found that most of the children who suffer from child leukaemia stay far away from power lines

(C) the number of potential ailments, i.e. over 1000, was so large that it created a high probability that at least one ailment would exhibit statistically significant difference just by chance alone

(D) there was no significant correlation between the other 999 diseases and how close to power lines a person stayed

(E) child leukaemia, unlike leukaemia in adults, can be cured by medicines and therapy and is rarely fatal

34) The mayor of Newtown is up for re-election in a month's time and is extremely apprehensive of his chances. According to a recent survey conducted by a news channel in Hampstead, Newtown's most populous suburb, more than 80 percent of the respondents stated that they would not vote for the current mayor.

The mayor's apprehensions are based on which of the following assumptions?

(A) The people who were part of the survey will in no case change their mind.

(B) The opinion of the residents of Hampstead is a pretty accurate representation of the opinion of the residents of Newtown as a whole

(C) The mayor was recently involved in a corruption scandal that received a lot of negative publicity in the print media

(D) The mayor did not do enough to help the victims of the hurricane that struck Newtown last year

(E) In the last three elections for the post of the mayor in Newtown, the incumbent mayor has never been re-elected to office

35) **The government has recently been severely criticized for its decision to block access to a few websites** on which malicious information and photographs were being posted. The government has responded to this criticism by stating that **while it believes in freedom of speech and expression, this was an emergency** and in such situations, you have to cut off the source of the problem.

In the argument given, the two portions in boldface play which of the following roles?

(A) The first describes a reaction to an action and the second describes an action taken in response to this reaction

(B) The first is a criticism that the argument disagrees with; the second is the point of view that the argument supports

(C) The first is the point of view of a group of people and the second attacks this point of view

(D) The first provides a counterpoint to the argument's conclusion; the second is that conclusion

(E) The first provides the criticism of an action and the second provides justification for the necessity of taking that action

36) Customer reviews are becoming a fixture on retail and consumer brand websites, with over 70% of retailers planning to feature them by the end of the year. The accelerated adoption of customer reviews indicates a more enlightened approach to handling negative comments—that is, the acknowledgment that occasional negative reviews do not hurt sales.

Under which of the following conditions is the above strategy likely to backfire?

(A) The quality of the product in question is so poor that a customer is not likely to buy it in the first place

(B) There are frequent negative reviews for a product

(C) The 20% of the retailers who do not launch this feature decide to offer huge discounts on their products

(D) The customers of a product never come to know about the existence of this feature on the product website

(E) It costs retailers a considerable sum of money to implement this feature on their respective websites

37) A new study provides more support for the hypothesis that social support may strengthen people's immune system. This study actually found that social isolation and loneliness can impair the immune system. According to the findings of the study, lonely and socially-isolated first-year students mounted a weaker immune response to the flu shot than other students.

The argument is flawed primarily because

(A) it assumes that there can only be one cause for an effect

(B) it assumes that a necessary condition for an event is a sufficient condition for that event to occur

(C) it assumes that if a cause for an effect is removed, then the effect will in turn get reversed

(D) it mistakes a symptom for a cause

(E) it is based on unverified and subjective data

38) For the past two decades, Eton Coaching Institute has been the market leader in preparing students for the entrance test to medical schools in the country. While several new players have set up shop in the last few years and have shown good results, it remains without doubt that if a student wishes to ace the medical school entrance test, his best chances are with Eton Coaching Institute.

The statements above, if true, best support which of the following assertions?

(A) There is something unique about the books provided by the Eton Coaching Institute that makes its students perform well in the medical school entrance test.

(B) If a student does not join the Eton Coaching Institute, he will most likely fail to clear the medical school entrance test.

(C) The teachers at Eton Coaching Institute are probably better than those at other institutes

(D) A student could clear the medical school entrance test, even if he hasn't prepared with the Eton Coaching Institute

(E) If a student has prepared with the Eton Coaching Institute, he will clear the medical school entrance test.

39) It is extremely unlikely that the incumbent governor will be voted back to office in the coming elections. According to a recent survey of residents of the state, more than 80% expressed dissatisfaction with the governor's performance and almost 60% stated that they would vote for the governor's opponent.

Which of the following most strongly supports the argument?

(A) The views of most of the state's residents are in concordance with the views of the survey's respondents

(B) The governor has received a lot of bad publicity in the past owing to his involvement in a corruption scandal

(C) The survey covered only a small fraction of the state's populace

(D) The governor's opponent is very popular amongst the residents of the state

(E) The newspapers in the state are against the governor and favour his opponent instead

40) The decision to ban the use of hands free mobile phone headsets while driving is not justified. There is no doubt that mobile phone use while driving is distracting and dangerous. However, it is dangerous because drivers use their hands and eyes to operate the phone, when their full physical attention should be on the road. Hands-free technologies allow for mobile phone use without such distractions, and these options should remain legal.

Which of the following, if true, undermines the argument above?

(A) The functioning of the eyes and the hands is governed by the brain and there is considerable evidence to show that the use of mobile phones distracts the brain

(B) Most good quality hands free headsets are expensive which will discourage people from buying them

(C) Just because something is legal does not necessarily mean that it is safe

(D) There have been some incidents of road accidents involving drivers who were talking on the mobile phones using hands free technology while driving at the time of the accident

(E) There are other technologies available, such as the use of Bluetooth to connect one's mobile phone to the car's speaker system, that are much safer than the use of hands free devices

41) Researchers from a data analysis firm have found that the three most popular combinations -- 1234, 1111, and 0000 -- account for close to 20 per cent of all four-digit passwords. The researchers also found that every four-digit combination that starts with 19 ranks above the 80th percentile in popularity, with those in the upper 1900s coming in the highest. Also quite common are combinations in which the first two digits are between 01 and 12 and the last two are between 01 and 31.

If the statements above are true, which of the following must be true?

(A) The password 1922 will most likely be less popular than 1981

(B) The password 0123 will most probably be more common than 2331

(C) If a password was to be selected from a random list of 100 four digit passwords, there is a very high possibility that it will be 1234, 1111, or 0000

(D) One out of three four digit passwords will be 1234, 1111, or 0000

(E) Passwords starting with 19 are more popular than those starting with 21

42) People in medieval times believed that lice were beneficial for their health, because there hardly used to be any lice on people who were unwell. The reasoning was that the people got sick because the lice left. The real reason however is that lice are extremely sensitive to body temperature. A small increase of body temperature, such as in a fever, will make the lice look for another host.

If the above statements are all true, then what was wrong with the reasoning of people in medieval times about the connection between lice and disease?

(A) They assumed that nothing else could lead to the disease except the lice

(B) They assumed that a correlation was actually a cause and effect relation

(C) They assumed that the sample size that they saw was representative of the entire population at that time

(D) They mistook the cause of something for its effect

(E) They assumed without warrant that a necessary condition is most definitely also going to be a sufficient one.

43) Which of the following best completes the passage below?

Over the years, supporters of slavery have put forward several view-points to rationalize their belief. One such argument states that some people are meant to be slaves as part of the natural order of the universe, or as part of God's plan, and it is wrong to interfere with this by abolishing slavery. However, such an argument is flawed, because it fails to take into account the fact that ____________________.

(A) slavery is a cruel practice that does not find much favour with most people in this world

(B) just because something is part of God's plan does not mean it is the morally correct thing to do

(C) slavery is considered illegal in almost all the countries of the world

(D) there exist no certain criteria to distinguish between natural slaves and those who should not be enslaved

(E) just because something is meant to be does not mean that it has to be

44) The list of the highest paying cities in the world is headed by cities in Switzerland. This serves to reaffirm the fact that people in Western European cities on average earn three times more than those in Eastern Europe. The fact that, in Switzerland, deductions from salary are relatively low, further widens the gap between net wage level earned there and in other countries, especially in the rest of Western Europe. The largest wage differences are in Asia, where the highest value (Tokyo) is twelve times higher than the lowest (Delhi).

Which of the following can properly be inferred from the statements above?

(A) The Swiss pay less money in taxes than do people in the rest of Western Europe

(B) Delhi is the poorest city in the Asian continent

(C) The wage difference between the richest and poorest cities of Eastern Europe is less than twelve times

(D) Switzerland is not situated in Western Europe

(E) Tokyo has more rich people than does Delhi

45) The perceived value of goods and services, rather than just their price, is becoming an increasingly prominent factor in the purchase decisions of modern consumers, a new report has indicated. Thus it can be concluded that consumers will be increasingly willing to spend extra on goods and services that are high-quality and durable.

For the above statements to be true, which of the following must be true?

(A) The price of a product plays no role in the making of purchase decisions by modern consumers

(B) There is a positive relation between the quality of a product and its durability

(C) The modern consumer is not likely to allow the quality of a product to determine his purchase decision

(D) The ideal way for manufacturers to charge more for their products is to increase the perceived value of their products in the minds of the modern consumer

(E) The durability of a product is in some way related to its perceived value in the minds of modern consumers

46) There has been a sudden spurt in the cases of suicide amongst teenagers in Tango city. On investigation, a public interest group discovered that all of these teenagers had been listening to songs by an alternative rock group, The Demons, at the time of committing suicide. When the public interest group listened to the songs by this rock group, they were aghast to hear lyrics that encouraged people to kill themselves. Accordingly, the city mayor has decided to ban the sale and download of all alternative rock band albums in Tango city with immediate effect.

Which of the following, if true, would most strongly support the position above?

(A) Songs with lyrics that encourage people to kill themselves can actually lead to people killing themselves

(B) Alternative rock groups other than The Demons also contain lyrics that encourage people to kill themselves

(C) It is not required to impose a similar ban on movies containing large scale violence and bloodshed

(D) If people don't listen to songs by The Demons, they will not kill themselves

(E) It is the responsibility of a mayor to protect the citizens of his city

47) The 17 countries of the Eurozone are all united by one currency - the euro, but that doesn't mean that there aren't price disparities in the continent. A sum of 20 Euros can buy you 35 cups of coffee in Portugal but only 7 cups of coffee in Greece. The same amount of money can get you 16 cartons of eggs in Malta, but only 7 cartons of eggs in Ireland.

Which of the following conclusions can most properly be drawn from the information above?

(A) On an average, a cup of coffee costs more in Portugal than in Greece

(B) A carton of eggs costs more in Malta than in Ireland

(C) Price disparities are an unusual phenomenon in the countries of the Eurozone

(D) The cost of a cup of coffee in Greece is the same as that of a carton of eggs in Ireland

(E) Portugal is a cheaper country to stay in than is Greece

48) John, a stock broker, has a list of companies whose shares he recommends his clients to invest in. Over the past one year, the share price of 20 companies listed on the stock exchange has appreciated by 100% or more and 16 of these companies are part of John's list. Thus John claims that he is an expert at picking stocks and that more and more investors should park their funds with him to get the maximum return on their investment.

The answer to which of the following questions would be most important in determining whether an investor should park his funds with John?

(A) How many companies are there on John's list?

(B) Whether any other stock broker has also showed similar or better performance last year?

(C) What is the total number of companies listed on the stock exchange?

(D) Has John shown similar results in the previous years as well?

(E) Does John hire the services of someone else to identify stocks in which his clients should invest?

49) Which of the following best completes the passage below?

Measured globally, car use will go on rising, for as people in emerging markets get rich, they want the mobility and status that car-ownership offers. But in the rich world the decades-long link between rising incomes and car use has been severed and miles driven per person have been falling. This does not, however, warrant the conclusion that automobile manufacturers located in rich countries should brace themselves for tough times ahead, since ____________________.

(A) a reduction in car use does not necessarily indicate a reduction in car sales

(B) fears about smog and global warming have led many people in rich countries to prefer the use of public transport to that of private cars

(C) fuel prices are expected to increase further in the next few years

(D) there are several new car launches lined up in rich countries over the next couple of years

(E) relatively poorer countries will then probably generate even lower car sales

50) For a broadband company, reliability and low cost are two prime issues. CBC Broadband Company has faced reliability issues over the past 6 months leading to a lot of its users shifting to other companies. To counter this, CBC has decided to offer very low subscription rates for new customers. This strategy will most likely prove successful in getting new customers to register for CBC's broadband service because CBC does not have any online public forum on which its customers can air their grievances, so the new customers will be unaware of the problems faced by CBC's existing customers.

Which of the following, if true, most seriously calls into question the explanation above?

(A) Any contact between CBCs existing customers and its target customers is extremely unlikely

(B) CBCs competitors have not faced any serious problems of reliability in the past six months

(C) There exist popular avenues apart from company owned online public forums on which customers unhappy with a company's service can air their grievances

(D) The government has passed strict laws that impose heavy penalties on companies that do not fulfil promises that they make to customers

(E) The reliability of CBCs broadband service is not expected to improve in the near future.

51) According to a recent survey conducted in the US, about 52.5 per cent of Americans are now owners of at least some type of a mobile phone device. Interestingly, the same survey also found that 66 per cent of Asian community in the US owns smart phones, making Asians the leading users of such devices in the country.

Which of the following conclusions can most properly be drawn from the information above?

(A) More Asians own mobile phones than Americans

(B) The Asian community owns the maximum number of mobile phones in the US

(C) Almost half the population of the US does not own smart phones

(D) Feature phones sell more in the US than do smart phones

(E) The Asian community in the US is very well off which is why they can afford the more expensive smart phones

52) The Georgetown Public School recommends that all its students take an active interest in playing chess. This is because, according to a recent medical study, those students who played chess on an average performed better in tests of general intelligence than those who did not play chess. Thus the school contends that playing chess will boost up the intelligence of its students.

Which of the following raises the most serious doubt about the conclusion above?

(A) Some students who perform well in tests of general intelligence do not play chess

(B) Intelligent students are the only ones who take an interest in playing chess

(C) A similar correlation has not been observed with regards to other sports such as baseball

(D) Some of the students who play chess perform poorly in subjects such as History

(E) There can be other ways in which a student could develop intelligence

53) George: The anti-drunk driving campaigns will not be successful. Some people are just immune to these campaigns and will drink and drive no matter what.

Shelly: Complete eradication of drunk driving is not the expected outcome. The goal is reduction.

Shelly responds to George by

(A) questioning the veracity of George's evidence

(B) suggesting that George's conclusion is based on incorrect assumptions

(C) partially agreeing with the main conclusion of George but disagreeing with his reasoning

(D) partially agreeing with George's point of view but suggesting that he has overlooked a beneficial effect

(E) contradicting George's reasoning and supplying an alternative reasoning

54) Despite all the science and massive budgets involved in modern sports, many sportsmen and women at all levels of sport swear by superstitions or elaborate event rituals to enhance their game. Irrational as it may sound, these superstitions clearly boost performance because almost all the top sportspersons across the world have some superstition or the other that they always adhere to.

Which of the following would most help evaluate the conclusion that superstition clearly helps sportspersons?

(A) Whether sportspersons who are not as successful also have superstitions

(B) Whether there is empirical proof that superstition boosts the performance of sportspersons

(C) Whether sportsperson who don't have any superstitions are also as successful as the ones who do

(D) Whether superstition helps boost an individual's self belief dramatically

(E) Whether all successful sportspersons across the world have some superstition

55) The proposal requiring mutual fund companies to set aside a part of their fee for investor education is laudable but meaningless. The challenge actually lies in finding the right ways of educating investors and making them financially literate.

Which of the following, if true, most strongly supports the argument?

(A) People looking to invest in mutual funds currently lack the knowledge to make informed decisions

(B) Most mutual funds have accumulated large reserves of cash for investor education

(C) Investing in mutual funds is very different from investing in other financial instruments such as shares and debentures

(D) Financially literate customers, on the whole, provide more business to mutual fund companies than do financially ignorant ones

(E) Activities aimed at educating customers cost a lot of money and most mutual funds do not have the cash reserves to conduct such activities

56) Food colouring can be a form of deception if it is used to make people think that a fruit is riper, fresher, or otherwise healthier than it really is. This is because bright colours give the subconscious impression of healthy, ripe fruit, full of antioxidants and phytochemicals. A variation of this strategy is to use packaging which obscures the true colour of the foods contained within, such as red mesh bags containing yellow oranges or grapefruit, which then appear to be a ripe orange or red.

Which of the following must be true on the basis of the statements above?

(A) When buying fruits one must check the actual colouring of the fruit and not of its packaging

(B) Food colouring is not always done with the intention of deceiving people

(C) Consumers should avoid purchasing fruits wrapped in mesh bags because this most likely suggests that the something is wrong with the fruit

(D) Bright colouring is an accurate method of judging the freshness of a fruit

(E) The presence of phytochemicals in a fruit will most likely dissuade consumers from buying that fruit

57) In an election, Candidate A received 70% of the total votes cast and Candidate B received the remaining 30% of the total votes cast. Thus Candidate A was declared the winner. Candidate B has disputed the results of the election saying that he is much more popular with the public than is Candidate A.

Which of the following, if true, most helps to explain why Candidate B lost the election, despite being more popular than Candidate A?

(A) The public has been opposed to some of the policies of candidate B

(B) Candidate A had recently been in the news because of his involvement in a corruption scandal

(C) Most of candidate B's supporters are factory workers whose work shift time clashes with the time of the day when election votes can be cast

(D) The voting was conducted in an extremely fair manner with no incidents of cheating reported from anywhere

(E) Candidate A spent more time canvassing for votes than did Candidate B

58) The airfares on almost all routes in the country have increased considerably in the past six months. In fact, on some routes, the fares have as much as doubled from what they were six months earlier. Since there has been no significant increase in the number of fliers in the country in the last six months, the media has blamed cartelization in the airline industry for this rapid increase in fares.

Which of the following, if true, undermines the argument above?

(A) The media is known to sensationalise events of public importance to gain more readership/viewership

(B) The airfares on some routes have actually fallen over the past six months

(C) Two of the six airline companies operating within the country have shut down operations in the last six months

(D) The price of aviation fuel increased drastically two years back and has remained at that level since then

(E) Other neighbouring countries have also seen similar rise in air fares but nobody has accused the airline companies in those countries of cartelization

59) Clerical workers show more signs of stress during the work day than those in executive or higher positions. According to the findings of a study, employees on the lower levels of job hierarchy had higher blood pressure and increased heart rate in the mornings. They also had higher average levels of the stress hormone Cortisol throughout the day.

Each of the following is an assumption in the argument, EXCEPT:

(A) The study is representative of all employees in general

(B) High blood pressure cannot be caused by factors other than stress

(C) The hormone Cortisol does not itself cause stress

(D) Increased heart rate is a sign of stress

(E) The higher average salary and in general better lifestyle of the employees at the executive and higher positions to an extent insulates them from stress

60) Which of the following best completes the passage below?

Those who suggest that higher education should be offered to all for free are wrong. The cost of providing higher education will most likely be more than its benefits. Many vocational jobs require apprenticeships and in-house training, rather than a college degree. In fact, this would likely further exacerbate the unemployment issue, since ___________________.

(A) there would be no way for government to recover the extra money that it has spent on providing free higher education

(B) there are more vocational jobs available currently than jobs requiring higher education

(C) there would simply be more qualified candidates vying for the same number of jobs

(D) the sole purpose of higher education should not be to get jobs

(E) the population of people in the working age group is expected to grow rapidly in the coming years

61) Historical data for all the elections held in Gangnam City shows that all winning candidates have canvassed for at least 100 hours. In fact candidates who have canvassed for fewer than 100 hours have never ever won. Out of all the candidates contesting in the upcoming elections in Gangnam City, Candidate A has canvassed for 120 hours, Candidate B has canvassed for 150 hours, and Candidate C has canvassed for 90 hours.

If the statements above are true, which of the following conclusions is most strongly supported by them?

(A) Candidate B will most likely win the election

(B) Candidate C will most likely lose the election

(C) The winner of the election will either be Candidate A or Candidate B

(D) The results of an election cannot be solely dependent on how many hours a candidate canvasses for.

(E) If no other Candidate has canvassed for more than 150 hours, then Candidate B will win the election

62) A stain-removing agent currently available in City X can remove the most stubborn of stains from clothes but is not very popular because it leaves behind a foul smell in clothes. It takes around ten days for the smell to completely go away from the clothes. Another stain-removing agent has just been launched in City X which is as effective at cleaning stains as the older one. An advantage of the new stain-removing agent is that its smell starts to go away from the clothes in two days itself. Thus this new agent should easily be able to outsell the older one.

Which of the following pieces of information would be most helpful in evaluating the above argument?

(A) the rate of growth or decline in sales of stain-removing agents in city X

(B) the total number of stain removing agents sold last year in city X

(C) the per capita income of people residing in city X

(D) the amount of time it takes for the smell of the new stain-removing agent to completely go away from the clothes.

(E) a comparison of the smell of the new stain removing agent with that of similar agents available in other cities

63) While cooking pasta, most Italian chefs add some cooking oil. The reason for this is not difficult to ascertain. Oil by nature is a greasy substance so the use of cooking oil prevents the pasta from sticking to the utensil it's being cooked in.

Which of the following, if true, most seriously calls into question the explanation above?

(A) The oil used most often by Italian chefs in cooking is olive oil, which has a neutral taste

(B) While it is being cooked, the pasta never comes in contact with the oil

(C) There are some Italian chefs who do not use cooking oil while cooking pasta

(D) If added in large quantities, the cooking oil can spoil the taste of the pasta

(E) To provide added taste is not the reason why cooking oil is added to pasta while it is being cooked

64) A survey recently conducted at the Global Business School has thrown up two interesting findings.

Finding 1: In the last ten years, students attending Professor James' Economics classes were more likely to score in the top 10% of the class than were other students

Finding 2: In the last ten years, most of the students who scored in the top 10% of the class did not take classes from Professor James.

If the statements above are true, which of the following must be true?

(A) The quality of classes conducted by Professor James has probably decreased

(B) The number of students not taking classes from Professor James has increased over the last ten years

(C) There must be some factor other than attending Professor James' classes that can also make a student perform well in the subject

(D) The overall quality of the students who have joined Global Business School in the last ten years has increased

(E) Professor James needs to change his teaching methods if he wants more students to attend his classes

65) Cyber security experts have warned that accessing the internet through mobile phones is much more dangerous than accessing the internet through a regular computer. A computer system has more resources and more storage, and you can use security software to protect it. However, this is not the case with mobile phones, which have limited storage and, therefore, limited capacity for security software.

If the statements above are true, which of the following is the best way to make mobile phones more secure?

(A) Launch new security software with enhanced features that can provide better protection to mobile phones

(B) Avoid browsing the internet through mobile phones as much as possible

(C) Use calling software such as Skype that allows people to make calls from a computer itself

(D) Not use mobile phone internet to carry out confidential activities such as internet banking

(E) Increase the storage capacity of mobile phones

66) The apex banking regulator in the country has stated that banks are favouring profits over customer welfare. This is because banks are not passing on the benefit of cut in policy rates to the borrowers. The regulator regretted that the lending rates of banks have not come down in tandem with reduction in the liquidity reserve ratio rate; rather the rates have gone up.

Which of the following, if true, is most damaging to the position taken by the apex banking regulator?

(A) Banks are in essence businesses so their primary motive should be to make profits

(B) The costs of running a bank have gone up considerably in recent times

(C) Many banks still invest a considerable amount of money in improving the banking experience of their customers

(D) The sales of several high value products such as automobiles and homes have gone down because of the high interest rate charged on loans by banks

(E) Even publicly owned banks have not passed on the benefit of lower liquidity reserve ratio rates to their customers

67) David Spiegel stunned the world in 1989 when he revealed that certain therapy groups may help breast cancer patients live longer. These groups also seem to help them live better. So if you suffer from breast cancer there is a good chance that you can improve your life, and maybe even extend it, by joining a professionally led support/therapy group that uses Spiegel's "supportive-expressive" model.

If the statements above are true, which of the following conclusions is most strongly supported by them?

(A) It would be a good idea for cancer patients to be part of some support or therapy group

(B) Being part of a support/therapy group increases a breast cancer patients desire to get better

(C) One way of curing breast cancer is to make the patient join a support/therapy group

(D) Being part of a support/therapy group can have beneficial effects for certain groups of people

(E) Doctors recommend joining support/therapy groups as a means to alleviate the discomfort caused by breast cancer

68) Most people erroneously believe that airplanes are dangerous modes of transport. Statistics clearly reveal that more people are killed every year in road accidents than in air crashes. So travelling by airplanes is in fact safer than travelling by a car or a bus.

Which of the following, if true, most strongly supports the above explanation?

(A) Airlines across the globe spend significant amounts of money every year on adding new safety features to their airplanes

(B) There is no country in the world in which the number of people killed in air crashes exceeds the number of people killed in road accidents

(C) In a recently conducted survey by an independent agency, a majority of the respondents stated that they felt safer while travelling by air than while travelling by road

(D) The number of people who travel by airplanes every year is roughly equal to the number of people who travel by road.

(E) The technology used in modern aircrafts is much more sophisticated than that used in most forms of road transport.

69) The government is aiming to roll out an ambitious project of providing free medicines to its citizens at public health facilities across the country. Once the scheme is launched, the government will provide free generic medicines to all patients coming to public health facilities. Opponents of the project have criticized it, stating that since the plan covers only generic medicines, most of the citizens will be outside its purview.

Which of the following, if true, would most weaken the criticism made above of the Health Ministry's strategy?

(A) The Health Ministry has made suitable arrangements to ensure that there is no shortage of generic drugs once the new scheme is rolled out

(B) A survey of public health facilities across the country has revealed that more than half of the prescribed medicines at these facilities comprise generic medicines

(C) Most of the country's citizens prefer branded medicines to generic ones

(D) The middle and lower income groups, which comprise a large chunk of the country's population, still frequent public health facilities to resolve their health issues

(E) The cost of running this scheme will eventually have to be borne by the citizens in the form of increased taxes

70) Jimmy's colleagues at work have noted that the days on which he comes to office by his car, he is in a very good mood and the days on which he comes to office by his bike he is in a grumpy mood. When Jimmy is in a grumpy mood his efficiency falls by almost fifty percent. Jimmy is currently working on a very important project that requires him to work at full efficiency. Therefore, his colleagues have suggested that Jimmy drive to work every day until the project is complete.

Which of the following would it be most useful to determine in order to evaluate the argument?

(A) Whether there is some other way using which Jimmy's efficiency can be increased

(B) Whether being in a good mood makes Jimmy want to drive to work

(C) Whether the bike is actually the reason for Jimmy's bad mood

(D) Whether Jimmy is unhappy with his working conditions

(E) Whether some other staff member can take Jimmy's place on the current project

71) There should be a ban on television commercials for prescription drugs. These commercials put preconceived notions in people's heads and make them ask for a drug from their doctor whose side effects they are not aware of. If a person needed that drug their doctor would have already known to prescribe it for him.

If the statements above are true, which of the following must be true?

(A) Most people who visit a doctor are already aware what drug the doctor will most likely prescribe to them

(B) Television commercials for prescription drugs don't have an educational aspect to them in that they don't educate the consumers about the use of various drugs

(C) Pharmaceutical companies try to sell harmful drugs to consumers by using deceptive advertising

(D) At least some people ask doctors to recommend to them medicines whose advertisement they have seen on television

(E) Doctors themselves at times use the advertisements for prescription drugs as a source of information to recommend medicines to their patients

72) It is interesting to note that, of the ten different brands of digital cameras available in the market, the one that sells the most is the second most expensive of the lot. This camera also offers the best picture quality of all the digital cameras available in the market. Clearly the price of the camera plays no role in the customer purchase decision; it is the picture quality of the camera that matters to customers.

Which of the following, if true, would most seriously weaken the argument above?

(A) Between two similarly equipped digital cameras, most customers will prefer the lower priced one

(B) There is a direct correlation between the price of a camera and its picture quality

(C) Some customers only purchase the cheapest available digital camera, irrespective of its picture quality

(D) The second largest selling brand of digital camera, which is also the third most expensive in the market, offers poor picture quality

(E) Digital cameras are usually purchased by affluent customers for whom the price of the camera isn't a big consideration

73) Telecom subscriber: It seems that all the telecom companies in our country are working in an absolutely unprofessional manner. The online consumer complaint forum is full of negative comments about all these companies, irrespective of the brand, while there are hardly any positive comments.

Telecom company representative: But this is because the people who are happy with our service don't have any incentive to post comments.

The telecom company representative responds to the telecom subscriber's complaint by

(A) raising doubts about the source of the customer's evidence

(B) pointing out that the customer has ignored the positive reviews that telecom companies get

(C) highlighting that the evidence in question is not representative of the entire population

(D) agreeing with the subscriber's conclusion but contradicting his use of evidence

(E) providing evidence that raises doubts over the claims made by the telecom subscriber

74) In a recent study of people afflicted by the Babblers syndrome an interesting fact was noted. The people suffering from this syndrome consumed dairy products in much larger quantities than people who were not suffering from this syndrome. Thus the study concluded that to reduce the chances of getting afflicted with Babblers syndrome, one should completely avoid the consumption of dairy products or consume them in moderate quantities at best.

The study's conclusion is based on which of the following assumptions?

(A) Excessive consumption of dairy products can have a negative impact on the health of people

(B) Babblers syndrome is a dangerous disease

(C) The effects of Babblers syndrome do not include excessive desire to consume dairy products

(D) Cutting down on dairy products will ensure that one does not contract Babblers syndrome

(E) Nothing else can lead to Babblers syndrome except the consumption of dairy products

75) Which of the following most logically completes the argument?

It is now known that to get the maximum out of a car engine one can do two things - use high octane fuel, which contains additives that extend the life and efficiency of the engine, or get the engine flushed at regular intervals, which removes all harmful substances from the engine. It has been shown by several studies that the use of high octane fuel is up to three times more effective in extending the life of the car engine than is the use of engine flushing. This does not, however, mean that engine flushing can play no role in extending the life of a car engine, because ______________.

(A) some studies have shown that using high octane fuel can lead to problems with a car's exhaust system

(B) high octane fuel costs much more than regular fuel and this cost is expected to increase even further over the next few years

(C) many car mechanics recommend the use of engine flushing over the use of high octane fuels

(D) the benefits of using high octane fuel are independent of the benefits of engine flushing.

(E) engine flushing, when not done by expert mechanics, can cause permanent damage to the engine of a car

76) The recent proposal by the government to introduce new conditions in the labour laws is a big setback to the IT industry in the US, especially at a time when it was expecting simplification of the currently applicable conditions. One of the proposed conditions, for instance, is that employers will have to disclose the names and locations of the clients hiring their workers, which will put them in automatic violation of non-disclosure agreements that are the norm in any contract.

Which of the following conclusions can most properly be drawn from the information above?

(A) The non-disclosure agreement bars IT companies from revealing the names of their employees working with different clients in the US

(B) If the proposed conditions come into effect, IT companies will not be able to carry on their operations in the US without violating client non-disclosure agreements

(C) The US government's actions will lead to reduced profitability of IT companies operating in the US

(D) The US government's actions with regards to changes in the country's labour laws did not exactly come as a surprise for most IT companies

(E) The IT industry will most likely curtail operations in the US if the US government does not take back its newly imposed conditions

77) **Existing optical lenses are not thin or flat enough to remove distortions**, such as spherical aberration and astigmatism, which prevent the creation of a sharp image. Correction of those distortions requires complex solutions, such as multiple lenses that increase weight and take up space. To overcome these challenges, scientists have developed a new superthin, flat lens. **The surface of this lens is patterned with tiny metallic stripes which bend light differently as one moves away from the centre,** causing the beam to sharply focus without distorting the images.

In the argument given, the two portions in boldface play which of the following roles?

(A) The first states a problem with existing optical lenses and the second states the solution for this problem that has been developed by scientists

(B) The first is the main conclusion of the argument and the second provides support for this main conclusion

(C) The first is evidence the accuracy of which is questioned later in the argument; the second is a conclusion that the argument supports

(D) The first mentions a problem with existing optical lenses and the second describes the structure of a new type of lens that can solve that problem

(E) The first is a problem associated with one type of optical lens; the second advocates the use of an alternative lens

78) Ever since the new Marketing Head joined Crackwell Corporation, its profits have increased steadily. In fact, over the past three years that the Marketing Head has been with Crackwell, the company's profits have grown by almost 35% every year, a figure that used to hover around the 10% mark earlier. Pleased by this fact, the Board of Crackwell Corporation has decided to reward the Marketing Head with stock options in the company.

Which of the following, if true, casts the most serious doubts on the decision taken by the Board of Crackwell Corporation?

(A) The Marketing Head is disliked by his team members because of his habit of criticising them in public

(B) Over the past three years, the profits of Crackwell's closest competitor have grown by 42% every year

(C) The CFO of Crackwell Corporation has taken several cost cutting measures over the last three years, including retrenchment of unproductive employees and renegotiation of prices with vendors.

(D) A strategy consulting firm, known to have turned around several poorly performing companies, has been recently hired by Crackwell Corporation

(E) Several new marketing campaigns, which gave a lot of international exposure to the company's products, have been successfully conducted by Crackwell Corporation over the past three years

79) In a recent survey of shoppers in the United States, 8 out of 10 shoppers said that they notice "Made in the USA" tags on products and most of those shoppers claim that they are more likely to purchase a product after noticing this tag. These shoppers further stated that the primary reason they are more likely to buy these products is because they wish to support the US economy.

Which of the following does most to show that the shoppers mentioned in the argument may have in fact been lying about why they purchase products with 'Made in America' labels?

(A) There is no difference in the quality of products manufactured in USA and those manufactured abroad

(B) The products that these shoppers said they would purchase include food, medicine, and personal items – products for the purchase of which quality and safety are the overriding considerations and in general products made in the USA are perceived to be safer than those made outside the USA

(C) Some customers purchase products with the "Made in USA" tag because they find the quality of these products to be better than those manufactured in other countries

(D) The products that are made in the USA in most cases cost significantly more than those manufactured abroad

(E) A large proportion of shoppers, who were not part of this survey, stated that when they buy a product they do not look at its country of manufacture

80) Arguments to restrict immigration on the grounds that immigrants will take domestic jobs ignore the fact that immigrants, once employed, will earn and spend money on goods and services, creating new jobs that will more than make up for the old ones they took.

Which of the following is an assumption on which the argument depends?

(A) The immigrants will not send most of the money that they earn back to their hometowns

(B) Studies show that large scale inflow of immigrants invariably leads to an increase in the incidence of crime in that city

(C) The immigrants will not subsequently get their families to also join them in the new city

(D) Immigrants generally tend to save most of the money that they earn

(E) Opponents of immigration are not opposed to immigration for reasons other than loss of jobs

81) A subsidy is assistance paid to a business or an economic sector. Governments in developing countries provide subsidies to the general populace on several items such as fuel, cooking gas, etc. Of late such countries have faced a lot of criticism from the World Bank for continuing to offer these subsidies to their citizens. Nonetheless, given that elections are just around the corner in most of these countries, they are likely to continue offering these subsidies.

Which of the following inferences is best supported by the lines above?

(A) To win an election in a developing country, subsidies must be offered to the people

(B) Subsidies lead to inefficiencies in the economy of a nation

(C) Providing subsidies will improve the chances of the incumbent government coming back to power in the developing countries mentioned in the stimulus

(D) Developed countries do not provide any subsidies to their citizens

(E) Governments in developing countries favour appeasing people to achieving economic growth

82) Which of the following most logically completes the argument below?

Mobile phones emit radioactive radiation because they use radio frequency waves to make and receive calls. Even though the doses are very small, experts at the World Health Organisation (WHO) have voiced concern that these emissions might cause leukaemia and other diseases and have issued a warning against the excessive use of mobile phones. The WHO, then, is most likely going to issue a similar warning for home phones wired to a wall jack as well, because

________________ .

(A) home phones are also used to make and receive calls

(B) home phones are also communication devices used by the general public

(C) home phones also use radio frequency waves

(D) people, on an average, spend more time talking on home phones than on mobile phones

(E) experts have voiced concern about the use of home phones as well

83) **As pets have become increasingly humanised in recent years, almost becoming a substitute for children in some cases,** owners have become increasingly concerned about the quality of their pets' diets , leading to rising interest in grain-free offerings. **According to its critics, grain is merely a "filler" in pet food** that has little real nutritional benefit.

In the argument given, the two portions in boldface play which of the following roles?

(A) The first is the cause of a given effect; the second is a criticism of that effect

(B) The first is the cause of a given effect; the second is the opinion of a group that provides further support for this effect

(C) The first describes a general scenario and the second provides a specific implication of this scenario

(D) The first is the point of view of a group of people and the second contradicts this point of view by providing conflicting evidence

(E) The first is the conclusion of the argument and the second provides evidence on the basis of which this conclusion has been arrived at

84) I do not think it is right to project electric cars as better than gas-fuelled cars. One negative aspect of electric cars is the fact they don't have enough power and, as a result, enough acceleration to perform in certain driving situations. For example, this lack of power could be dangerous in driving situations when fast acceleration is needed to avoid an accident.

Which of the following, if true, would most seriously weaken the argument above?

(A) Electric cars are much better for the ecology than are gas fuelled ones

(B) Electric cars are much cheaper to run than are gas fuelled cars

(C) The price of fuel is only expected to increase in the future whereas the price of technology used in the manufacture of electric cars is expect to decrease

(D) The biggest reason for road accidents is over speeding, which is the direct result of increased power in a car

(E) In future, electric cars are expected to have much more powerful engines than do current electric cars

85) Photon city is known for its commerce colleges across the nation. However, it seems that the quality of education imparted at these colleges has deteriorated considerably with time. When commerce graduates living in Photon city were recently administered a test, most of them could not even answer simple questions such as what was meant by activity based costing.

The argument is most vulnerable to the criticism that

(A) it incorrectly assumes that all commerce graduates have to be aware of what is meant by activity based costing

(B) it makes no distinction between commerce graduates living in Photon city and those who have graduated from commerce colleges in Photon city

(C) it does not take other important skills such as interpersonal skills and communication skills into consideration

(D) it provides no details about how commerce graduates in the rest of the country have performed on this test

(E) it does not take into account the education policies of the government

86) The restrictions on what one can carry inside an airplane are surely too severe. Airlines these days issue a long checklist of items that cannot be carried inside an aircraft making it cumbersome for the travellers to keep a track of all these items. In any case barely two percent of travellers are ever caught with these restricted items, so it's best if these restrictions are removed.

Which of the following is an assumption on which the argument depends?

(A) The restrictions themselves do not discourage people from carrying restricted items on to airplanes

(B) The restrictions have been implemented all across the world

(C) There is no scope for corrupt practices on the part of those enforcing these restrictions

(D) There have been instances when an innocent traveller has been wrongly detained by over cautious airline personnel

(E) Criminals are hardly likely to carry restricted items with them on an airline

87) According to a research of 1000 individuals, 70% of the people who were part of Genco Slimming centre's weight loss program, lost an average of 4 pounds of weight in one month. However the same research also found that 80% of the people, who lost an average of 4 pounds of weight in that month, did not attend Genco Slimming centre's weight loss program.

Which of the following conclusions can most properly be drawn from the information above?

A. The number of people who were part of Genco's weight loss program is greater than the number of people who lost an average of more than 4 pounds of weight in that month

B. The people who did not join Genco's weight loss program and yet managed to lose an average of 4 pounds of weight in a month must have followed a very strict exercise regime of their own

C. The number of people who did not join Genco's weight loss program and who lost less than an average of 4 pounds of weight in the month is lower than the number of people who attended Genco's weight loss program and lost less than an average of 4 pounds of weight

D. The number of people who did not join Genco's weight loss program and who still managed to lose an average of more than 4 pounds of weight in that month is greater than the total number of people who joined Genco's weight loss program

E. The chances of a person losing an average of more than 4 pounds of weight in one month are higher if the person does not join Genco's weight loss program

88) It appears that the residents of Clarktown are becoming more and more health conscious these days. The sale of fitness equipment such as treadmills and cycling machines has increased by more than 300% in Clarktown over the last one year.

Which of the following, if true, casts the most serious doubt on the conclusion drawn above?

(A) Due to a change in the sales tax structure last year, fitness equipment costs up to 30% less in Clarktown than in its neighbouring towns.

(B) The sale of health magazines has increased appreciably in Clarktown over the past one year.

(C) Nutritionists in Clarktown have reported a sharp increase in the cases of obesity that have been reported in Clarktown over the past year.

(D) The range of fitness equipment available at Clarktown is very limited and some advanced machines are not available at all

(E) Two athletes, both of whom won gold medals at the Olympics three years ago, are residents of Clarktown

89) Researcher at Columbus Children's Hospital: **Migraines are common in children as are behavioural disorders such as attention deficit disorder (ADD), conduct disorder (CD) and oppositional defiant disorder (ODD).** We have now concluded that a direct relationship in fact exists between paediatric migraines and the behavioural disorder, ODD – one of the most common of the disruptive behavioural disorders occurring in children. **Children with migraines miss more school and often lose sleep,** factors which are known to contribute to the types of behavioural symptoms often associated with ODD,

In the argument given, the two portions in boldface play which of the following roles?

(A) The first is the main conclusion of the researcher and the second provides evidence supporting this main conclusion

(B) The first mentions terms, between the two of which the researcher later concludes exists a causal relation; the second is the basis for this conclusion

(C) The first is a general statement on the basis of which a conclusion is arrived at later in the argument; the second provides additional basis for this statement

(D) The first mentions terms, between the two of which the researcher later concludes exists a causal relation; the second is the basis for a secondary conclusion

(E) The first describes a possible correlation between migraine and certain other medical conditions and the second provides evidence suggesting that this correlation may in fact be a cause and effect relation

90) 30% of the residents of Tafta City own cars. However 70% of the residents of Hampton, a suburb in Tafta City, are car owners. So it can be concluded that the total number of cars owned by residents of Hampton exceeds the total number of cars owned by the rest of the residents of Tafta City.

The answer to which of the following questions would be most important in determining whether the above conclusion is correct?

(A) What is the total population of Tafta City?

(B) What proportion of the population of Tafta City resides in Hampton?

(C) What is the total number of cars owned by residents of Tafta City?

(D) What is the total number of people residing in Hampton?

(E) What proportion of the population of Tafta City has bought cars from outside Tafta City?

91) For people looking at purchasing laptops, there are two important decision parameters – the speed of the laptop's processor and the backup that its battery provides. Jake, an expert at computers, believes that, of the two determinants, processor speed is the more important one. Surprisingly he recommends that his friends buy the laptop with the longest battery backup.

Which of the following best explains the apparent contradiction between Jake's belief and his recommendation?

(A) Jack is aware that a laptop with a processor that is faster than any of the current processors will be launched within the next six months

(B) Jake is aware that for a lot of buyers, a third factor – the weight of the laptop – is more important than the other two factors

(C) All the laptops currently available in the market use the same processor

(D) Laptops with powerful batteries cost more than those with regular batteries

(E) Jake is probably not as much of an expert at computers as he likes to believe

92) It is truly a waste of time to attend college. Out of the ten richest people in the world at the moment, six are college dropouts. Thus, if one wants to become rich, then it makes sense to drop out of college and start one's own venture.

Which of the following, if true, casts the most serious doubt on the argument?

(A) Had the six people mentioned in the argument attended college, they may have been even richer than they are currently

(B) Attending college helps a person increase his or her social circle by making new friends

(C) Statistics reveal that 95% of all new ventures are most likely to fail

(D) The percentage of college dropouts who have gone on to become rich is several times smaller than the percentage of college graduates who have gone on to become rich

(E) Becoming rich is not the only measure of success, happiness is perhaps more important

93) Over the last few years that he has been travelling by the subway, Ricky has made an interesting observation. Every time the train is late by more than six minutes, it gets extremely crowded and Ricky finds it impossible to get a seat. In the last 6 years, it has never happened that the train arrived more than six minutes late and Ricky could find a place to sit.

Which of the following conclusions can most properly be drawn from the above statements?

(A) The number of people travelling by the subway has increased several times over the last few years

(B) If the train comes on time, Ricky will definitely get a place to sit

(C) If Ricky does not find a seat in the train, it must have arrived more than six minutes late

(D) The Transport Authority needs to urgently increase the frequency of subway trains

(E) If the train arrives more than six minutes late, Ricky will most likely not find a place to sit

94) The number of people in Denvo city who like to watch movies in multiplexes has apparently increased considerably. Over the last five years it has become difficult to find seats in most multiplexes in Denvo City.

Which of the following, if true, most seriously weakens the argument?

(A) Several blockbuster movies were released in the last five years

(B) Denvo city had seven multiplexes out of which three have shut down in the last five years

(C) Many residents of Denvo city have stated in a survey that they hate going out for movies.

(D) The ticket prices charged by multiplexes in Denvo city have fallen over the past five years

(E) It is very easy to find seats in multiplexes situated in the neighbouring Vento city

95) Researchers have long been trying to understand why the consumption of opium makes one sleepy. A group of researchers has recently concluded that opium is sleep inducing because it has soporific qualities.

Which of the following parallels the flaw in the reasoning above?

(A) The student performed poorly in the test because he did not study for it

(B) It is dark at night because of the absence of the sun

(C) The new car has a powerful engine so it must also have powerful brakes

(D) Aeroplanes are able to fly because of their aerodynamic shape

(E) The price of a company' stock has not appreciated because the company's stock price has remained stagnant

96) Banker: Our asset quality is fairly strong and has been improving in the past few quarters. But given our size, we cannot afford to allow any of our large accounts to turn non-performing. It would create havoc for us.

Which of the following must be true on the basis of the statements made by the banker above?

(A) The bank in questions must be a small sized bank

(B) If any of the bank's accounts become non performing, the bank will go bankrupt

(C) The bank does not mind if any of its smaller accounts turn non-performing

(D) The bank used to have assets of a poor quality a few quarters back

(E) One of the important factors that will determine the bank's performance is the quality of its large accounts

97) Opponents of the free market approach assert that the free market often fails to achieve maximum efficiency—that it sometimes wastes resources. They often cite the example of utility services. If there were free competition among utilities, it would lead to a lot of duplication—different companies putting up telephone and electric poles, waterlines, etc., side by side, which would be a waste. So they argue that it is important for government to restrict competition and thus correct market failures.

The answer to which of the following questions would help evaluate whether the opponents of free market theory are correct?

(A) Whether it is possible to procure items such as electric and telephone poles used by utility services at low prices

(B) Whether there is some other feasible way of solving the problem of duplication mentioned in the argument

(C) Whether following this strategy is likely to lead to formation of monopolies that can be then used to exploit consumers

(D) Whether free market is likely to have any detrimental effect on the economy of the country

(E) Whether the free market approach has been adopted by any other countries in the world

98) A proposal has recently been floated by the government to increase road use tax rates across the country. This will lead to an increase in operating costs for trucking companies, who will then most likely increase their freight rates. The higher freight rates will in turn lead to a consequent increase in the prices of goods and commodities of daily use such as vegetable and grocery items. Thus if the proposal is passed, it will actively contribute to inflation in the country.

Which of the following, if true, most strongly indicates that the logic of the prediction above is flawed?

(A) It assumes that there is no other way in which inflation can increase apart from increased road use taxes

(B) It mistakes a likely outcome for a confirmed outcome

(C) It resorts to addressing peripheral issues while ignoring the deeper fundamental problems with the economy

(D) It assumes that the inflation will not increase if the road tax is not increased

(E) It mistakes a correlation for a cause and effect relation

99) Board of ABC Company: Owing to the excellent performance of the company in the last four quarters under the leadership of the new CEO, the Board has decided to reward the CEO with a 50% bonus.

Shareholder of ABC Company: But last year ABC Company's sales grew by only 30%, which was the lowest amongst all its competitors.

Which of the following provides the most logical counter for the Board to offer to the shareholder?

(A) ABC Company's sales had fallen every year for the past three years

(B) The CEO cannot be personally held responsible for the low sales growth

(C) The CEO needs to be encouraged, else he may lose the motivation to increase the sales further

(D) The CEO has hired several middle managers at very high salaries leading to increased costs for the company

(E) The CEO has not made any remarkable changes to the production or marketing strategy of the company

100) In a college election Tom received 50% of the votes cast, Jim received 30% of the votes cast, and Joanna received the remaining 20% of the votes cast. Jim was eventually declared the winner of the election for the post of the college President.

Which of the following conclusions can most properly be drawn from the information above?

(A) There were only three candidates who stood for the election

(B) The college students most likely don't like Joanna

(C) Tom must have spent more time campaigning than Jim or Joanna did

(D) The number of votes received was not a criterion to decide who would be President

(E) There must be some criterion, other than the number of votes received, that also helps decide who would be President

Answers & Explanations

Q No.	Answer	Q No.	Answer	Q No.	Answer	Q No.	Answer
1	A	26	D	51	C	76	B
2	D	27	A	52	B	77	D
3	E	28	D	53	D	78	C
4	D	29	E	54	A	79	B
5	D	30	B	55	B	80	A
6	D	31	B	56	B	81	C
7	B	32	C	57	C	82	C
8	D	33	C	58	C	83	B
9	C	34	B	59	E	84	D
10	E	35	E	60	C	85	B
11	B	36	B	61	C	86	A
12	C	37	C	62	D	87	D
13	A	38	D	63	B	88	A
14	E	39	A	64	C	89	B
15	B	40	A	65	E	90	B
16	C	41	A	66	B	91	C
17	C	42	D	67	D	92	D
18	E	43	D	68	D	93	E
19	D	44	C	69	B	94	B
20	E	45	E	70	B	95	E
21	D	46	B	71	D	96	E
22	B	47	D	72	A	97	C
23	C	48	A	73	C	98	B
24	E	49	A	74	C	99	A
25	B	50	C	75	D	100	E

1) Financial Expert: Our country has a very high debt-to-GDP ratio and it's difficult for a country with a high debt-to-GDP ratio to grow in a dynamic manner. Moreover our debt is growing higher and that means inflation is getting worse. All in all, our country is badly managed these days.

Which of the following assertions is most strongly supported by the passage?

(A) High debt has an adverse impact on the inflation rate

(B) It is not possible for a badly managed country to grow in a dynamic manner.

(C) High level of debt is extremely detrimental to the growth of a country

(D) Growing inflation is the sign of a badly managed country

(E) Whatever growth is happening in this particular country cannot possibly be dynamic growth

Official Answer: A

Explanation

Since this is an Inference question, let's look at each option and eliminate.

A. The argument clearly states that increasing debt is worsening the inflation rate, so then A can definitely be inferred
B. Cannot necessarily be concluded. We don't even know what all things constitute a badly managed country, so then we definitely cannot conclude this.
C. We know that high level of debt to GDP ratio is detrimental for the growth of a country but from this we cannot necessarily conclude that high level of debt by itself is extremely detrimental. If the GDP is also high then high level of debt could be a good thing
D. This may not necessarily be true because the argument states that all the things together constitute a badly managed country, but what is true for the whole may not be true for each part
E. The argument states that it's *difficult* for this country to grow in a dynamic manner and not that it is *impossible* for this country to do so

2) In the early 1960s, Myanmar was the richest country in Asia, but then it closed its economy to the outside world and is now the poorest country in the region. However, Myanmar is now opening up its economy to the outside world once again, and so will soon regain its former glory. Thus it makes sense for smart investors to invest in Myanmar.

Which of the following is an assumption on which the argument depends?

(A) A closed economy will rapidly deplete the financial resources of a country

(B) The countries that dealt with Myanmar in 1962 will still be interested in dealing with it

(C) If Myanmar does not open up its economy to the outside world, it will continue to remain poor.

(D) The severe internal unrest that has continued in Myanmar for the last several years is not responsible for its current financial state.

(E) At least some smart investors are currently aware of Myanmar's past glory

Official Answer: D

Explanation

The argument concludes that the only reason why Myanmar became the poorest country in the Asian region is because it closed its economy to the outside world. Thus it assumes that there can be no other explanation for this fact. (D) is one such passive assumption, which has to be true for the conclusion to be true. If you negate (D) then the argument will fall apart.

A. This may be inferred from the argument but is definitely not an assumption
B. Doesn't necessarily have to be true. New countries may want to deal with Myanmar now.
C. Again this may be an inference but is not an assumption
D. The correct answer.
E. This is irrelevant to the argument

3) With less than 20 per cent market share, Cherico Airline has been steadily losing ground to other competing airlines. However, the recent addition of the Dreamliner aircraft to its fleet might just turn the tide for Cherico. The Dreamliner claims 15 per cent more fuel efficiency than competing similar aircrafts and cheaper maintenance costs. With the induction of these planes, Cherico will get a competitive advantage over its more aggressive rivals, which will be saddled with older aircrafts and get deliveries of their own Dreamliners only in 2014.

Which of the following would it be most useful to determine in order to evaluate the argument?

(A) Whether it is possible for Cherico to cut costs even more by reducing the number of stewards in the air plane

(B) Whether it is possible for Cherico to improve the Dreamliner's fuel efficiency even further by restricting the amount of luggage passengers can carry

(C) Whether Cherico can increase its revenues by charging for the meals it serves in its aircrafts

(D) Whether the Dreamliner's maintenance costs will be substantially lower than those of Cherico's rivals' aircrafts

(E) Whether it will be possible for Cherico's rivals to somehow get deliveries of their own Dreamliners expedited

Official Answer: E

Explanation

The whole argument is based on the assumption that Cherico's competitors will not be able to get the Dreamliner before 2014. If there was some way in which the competitors could also get their hands on the Dreamliner earlier, then Cherico's competitive advantage will get neutralized. (E) mentions this point and is the correct answer

A. It is possible that other airlines could also reduce the number of stewards in their airplanes. The argument is only concerned with the competitive advantage accruing due to the Dreamliner.
B. This may be an added advantage but the whole point of the argument is that the competitors will not be able to get their hands on the Dreamliner before 2014.
C. This has no bearing on the competitive advantage accruing due to the Dreamliner
D. The argument clearly states that this will be the case so this basically repeats what is already stated in the argument
E. The correct answer

4) G. Bell Corporation, a manufacturer of mobile handsets, has claimed to have become the leading seller of mobile handsets, in terms of units sold, in the country. According to latest figures released by all the handset manufacturers in the country, G. Bell Corporation managed to sell 80 per cent of the total handsets that it manufactured during the year whereas the market leader, H. Wells Corporation, managed to sell only 50 per cent of its total handsets.

Which of the following identifies a flaw in G. Bell Corporation's reasoning?

(A) It does not take into account H. Wells Corporation's huge book of advance orders for handsets that need to be shipped during the next year

(B) It incorrectly assumes that the current trend will continue into the next year as well

(C) It makes no comparison of the average price at which G. Bell Corporation sold its handsets with the average price at which H. Wells Corporation sold its handsets

(D) It does not take into account the total number of handsets sold by either manufacturer

(E) It does not take into account the total market size for mobile handsets in the country

Official Answer: D

Explanation

Note that the argument states that G. Bell sold 80% of its total production (and not of the total market size) and H. Wells sold 50% of its total production. For the conclusion to be true the argument has to assume that the total number of handsets manufactured by the two manufacturers are the same, but this may not be the case. (D) questions this fact and so is the correct answer.

A. Future sales are outside the scope of the argument. For all you know G. Bell could also have equally large advance order bookings
B. The argument assumes no such thing
C. The argument is concerned with units sold so the price is outside the scope
D. The correct answer
E. The total market size is again irrelevant because we don't know how much of the total market size each of the two manufacturers account for

5) The supply of iron ore, the most important component in steelmaking, has been steadily declining in Marco city. This has forced steel manufacturing units in Marco city to source iron ore from far off mines leading to an increase in their transportation costs. Because transportation costs make up a large chunk of the total cost of steelmaking, the steel manufacturers in Marco city have had no option but to increase the selling price of their steel. This has in turn led to an increase in the retail price of utensils and other articles of daily use made of steel. Since the retail consumers now have to pay more for these steel items, while their earnings remain unchanged, they have decided to cut down on their non essential expenditure such as that on movie tickets. This has led movie theatres in Marco city to reduce their ticket prices.

Which of the following provides the most support for the assertion that the prices of movie tickets in Marco city will continue to decline in future?

(A) The people of Marco city will not be willing to cut down their expenditure on eating out

(B) After the inauguration of the Goldport Bridge, expected to happen very soon, the transportation costs to Marco city will be halved

(C) There are no blockbuster movies with stellar star casts lined up for release anytime soon

(D) The supply of iron ore to Marco city is expected to go down even more in the near future

(E) Residents of Marco city view movie tickets as non essential items of expenditure

Official Answer: D

Explanation

This argument consists of a series of cause and effects, wherein the effect of one event becomes the cause of another event. The last item in this chain is the reduction of movie ticket prices by movie theatres in Marco City. So one entire chain of cause and effect has ended with movie theatres lowering their ticket prices. Now why will the movie theatres lower their ticket prices even further? Only if the cycle of cause and effect were to start all over again and continue on and on. Since the cycle starts with the decline in supply of iron ore to Marco city, for the cycle to continue the supply of iron ore has to keep on decreasing in future as well. (D) states this and is the correct answer.

A. Unless we are told whether the expenditure on eating out is essential or non essential expenditure, this point will be irrelevant to the argument
B. This should actually weaken the argument by suggesting that the impact of reduced iron ore supply could be absorbed by the reduction in transport cost.
C. The presence of blockbuster movies is outside the scope of the argument
D. The correct answer
E. Even if this is so, the movie ticket prices should stabilize at their new low prices. Why should they go down further?

6) The Starbeans cafe has recently hired a new manager. The manager, within a few days of joining, made some drastic changes as a result of which the number of people visiting Starbeans everyday fell by almost 40%. However the revenue during this same period almost doubled.

Which of the following, if true, most helps to explain how the revenues of Starbeans increased despite the falling footfalls?

(A) The manager appointed a new coffee bean supplier who charges much lower rates than did the earlier supplier, resulting in substantial cost savings.

(B) The manager changed the interior of the cafe, making the seats much more comfortable than the earlier seats and adding more colour to the walls.

(C) The manager's monthly salary is directly linked to the revenue; the more the revenue the more salary he gets.

(D) The manager increased the average price of every item on the menu, in some cases even doubling the original price

(E) The manager fired some of the staff, thereby cutting down Starbean's salary cost by half.

Official Answer: D

Explanation

The only way in which revenues can increase despite a fall in the number of visitors is if the price per item were to be increased. (D) states this and is the correct answer. This also explains why the number of customers visiting Starbeans has gone down.

A. Low rates for coffee beans will reduce the cost and increase the profit, but it cannot increase the revenue
B. If anything, this fact should have helped increase the number of customers to Starbeans
C. This still does not explain how sales can increase despite falling customers
D. The correct answer
E. Same as A

7) According to a report by the American Staffing Federation (ASF), the government's new policy for the retail industry is likely to create 2 million jobs for fresh graduates over the next three years. The ASF has, thus, welcomed the government's move to implement this policy across the nation as its implementation will lead to a lowering of the national unemployment rate.

Which of the following, if true, would cast the most serious doubt on the accuracy of AFS' conclusion?

(A) Opponents of the policy will not allow the government to implement the policy anytime soon

(B) The new policy will result in a large number of uneducated workers becoming redundant and, as a result, losing their jobs

(C) There are several other ways of lowering the national unemployment rate available to the government

(D) The nation faces more serious problems than unemployment and the government should instead focus on resolving those first

(E) The implementation of the new policy is going to cost the government a considerable amount of money so the government will most likely increase corporate tax rates to recover this amount

Official Answer: B

Explanation

The argument concludes that the government's new policy to create jobs should be supported because it will create a large number of jobs for a particular group – fresh graduates. However, if there was evidence to show that this policy could lead to large scale job loss in another segment (uneducated workers), then the benefits of the policy would be negated. (B) does this and is the correct answer.

A. The question is not of whether the policy will actually be implemented or not but of whether the policy should be implemented
B. The correct answer
C. We are not concerned about the other ways but about whether this new policy should be that way
D. The other problems that a nation faces are outside the scope of the argument
E. The government might be willing to foot the cost if the returns are worth it, so this does not necessarily weaken the argument

8) It may soon be possible to insure your Facebook, Twitter, and other social media accounts against the nuisance of hacking as a company has launched the country's first social media insurance. The insurance includes the cost of disabling accounts, suppressing offensive material and stopping any legal action triggered by hacking, for example if a hacker posts illegal material under a victim's name.

Which of the following can properly be inferred from the statements above?

(A) Social media insurance will make it possible for individuals to sue hackers who post offensive content in their name

(B) The launch of social media insurance will, most likely, lead to a fall in the incidence of hacking on social media sites such as Facebook and Twitter

(C) There is a cost associated with enabling and disabling a social media account

(D) Under current laws it is possible for a person to be sued for posting offensive material online even if the person did not post the material himself

(E) Social media insurance will only be available for Facebook and Twitter users

Official Answer: D

Explanation:

Since this is an Inference question, let's look at each option and eliminate.

A. There is no connection between insurance and the ability to sue someone. Insurance will just compensate an individual for the damages incurred because of the acts of a hacker
B. This may or may not be the case but doesn't necessarily have to be the case.
C. We know there is a cost associated with disabling an account but we don't know whether there is a similar cost associated with enabling an account.
D. The correct answer. The argument states that social media insurance will stop any legal action triggered by a hacker posting something offensive in the user's name. Thus, under the current laws, it must be possible to sue a person for an offensive online act that he hasn't himself committed
E. The argument never states this; it just uses the example of Facebook and Twitter.

9) According to those in favour of privatisation of Social Security in the US, the current system is impossible to sustain. Decades ago, there were many more workers for every recipient but now the situation has reversed. Sooner or later, the fund will not be able to meet its obligations, because there will be more payments going out, than income coming in. Privatizing the system for the future recipients, while gradually phasing out the system for current and near-term recipients, is probably the best way to keep the system viable.

The answer to which of the following questions would be most useful in determining whether privatisation of Social Security in the US would be a good idea?

(A) Whether privatization has proved successful for other government provided services such as employee provident funds

(B) Whether the population of the US is likely to increase significantly in the future

(C) Whether the growth in the number of workers is the US is likely to outstrip the growth in the number of dependents in the future

(D) Whether privatization of social security will lead to large scale protests by US citizens

(E) Whether taking loans can help the Social Security system tide over the problem of the reduction in funds coming in to the system

Official Answer: C

Explanation

The argument assumes that in the US the number of dependents in the future will be far more than the number of earning workers, a situation that will lead to the social security funds drying up. However if this assumption is not true, then the social security system could continue working as it has been over the years. (C) points out this fact and is the correct answer.

A. Whether privatization has proved successful for other services has no bearing on whether privatization will work for the Social Security system
B. The problem is not the population growth rate but the ratio between earners and dependents. As long as this ratio remains favourable, an increase in population should not make any difference
C. The correct answer
D. This is not the basis of the argument's conclusion
E. Taking loans can provide a short term solution but the problem will remain in the long term

10) Large corporations use several strategies to minimize their tax payments, without doing anything explicitly illegal. One such strategy involves the use of transfer pricing, when subsidiaries in different countries charge each other for goods or services "sold" within the group. This is particularly popular among technology and drug companies that have lots of intellectual property, the value of which is especially subjective. These intra-company royalty transactions are supposed to be arm's-length, but are often priced to minimise profits in high-tax countries and maximise them in low-tax ones.

If the above statements are true, then which of the following could be a strategy adopted by a company that wants to get the maximum benefit out of transfer pricing?

(A) Sell its subsidiary located in a high tax rate country products at low prices

(B) Charge its subsidiary located in a low tax rate country higher prices for products sold

(C) Pay its subsidiary located in a high tax rate country high prices for products bought

(D) Pay its subsidiary located in a low tax rate country low prices for products bought

(E) Pay its subsidiary located in a low tax rate country high prices for products bought

Official Answer: E

Explanation

To get the maximum benefit out of transfer pricing, a company would want to show maximum earnings in a low tax country or minimum earnings in a high tax country. (E) states that the company would pay its subsidiary in a low tax country high prices i.e. the earnings of the subsidiary will be high and these will be taxed at a low rate, so the company will benefit overall.

A. When the company sells products it receives money. Since we have no idea about the tax rate in the country where the company is located, this option is irrelevant.
B. Same as (A). (When the company charges its subsidiary, it receives money)
C. If the company pays high prices to its subsidiary in a high tax rate country, the income of the subsidiary will be high and the tax on this income will also be high. So the company will lose money.
D. In this case, even though the subsidiary will pay lower taxes, its revenues will also be less because of the low prices charged.
E. The correct answer

11) Which of the following best completes the passage below?

When telecom companies, used to reporting several million new customers in a month, do the opposite and report a sharp fall in that number, you know that the country's most dynamic industry has entered a new, more troubled phase. However, this statistic may not necessarily be as much of a cause for concern as it looks because ______________________.

(A) mobile phone companies have huge cash reserves so they will not face the problem of cash flow for a few months at least

(B) inflated claims about new customer acquisition have been very much a part of the telecom industry story so far

(C) the sales of mobile phone handsets haven't fallen down appreciably

(D) other competitors have not entered the market in huge numbers

(E) mobile phone companies are making huge investments in widening their network coverage

Official Answer: B

Explanation

We have to somehow show that the statistics are not a sign for worry. (B) does this best by stating that the original statistics were most likely inflated so the fall in numbers may not actually be as steep as it looks.

A. But what about after a few months? This would still be a worrying sign for the companies
B. The correct answer
C. There is no real connection between the sale of mobile phone handsets and how many subscribers join mobile phone companies every month
D. If despite this fact the numbers are going down, then there must be some problem
E. This is irrelevant to the argument

12) The main purpose of business is to maximise shareholder value over the long term by selling goods or services. Thus, employees who use funds for anything other than to increase their sales are simply cheating the shareholders.

Which of the following is an assumption made in drawing the conclusion above?

(A) Most business owners would agree with the above definition of the purpose of a business

(B) Increasing sales is not the only way to maximise shareholder value

(C) Spending money on making the workplace more comfortable for employees will not lead to increased worker productivity and in turn increased business profits

(D) The only function of a business is to maximise returns for its shareholders

(E) According to this definition, many employees could be accused of cheating

Official Answer: C

Explanation

The argument assumes that the only way to maximise shareholder value is by increasing sales. This can lead us to several passive assumptions. (C) contains one such assumption. Notice that if you negate (C), the argument will fall apart.

A. Whether business owners agree with this definition is irrelevant
B. This weakens the argument whereas we need to find an assumption in the argument
C. The correct answer
D. This is directly stated in the argument so cannot be its assumption
E. This could be an inference but is definitely not an assumption

13) The prime principle of economics is that prices are determined by supply and demand, not by costs. Some products may cost 90 cents and sell for dollar, while others go for a dollar yet cost only a cent to make. The second producer is neither a profiteer nor an exploiter, and the first producer is neither a benefactor nor a patron. Both producers merely respond to market signals based on supply and demand.

If the statements above are true, which of the following must be true?

(A) How much it costs to manufacture a product is not the primary determinant of its selling price

(B) A product with a low manufacturing cost is more likely to succeed than a product with a high manufacturing cost

(C) A manufacturer who sells a product with a low manufacturing cost at a high price to the customer is deceiving the customer

(D) If a product costs a lot to manufacture then its manufacturer must ensure that he does not sell the product at a high price

(E) A manufacturer who uses manufacturing costs of a product as a basis to determine the selling price of the product is bound to fail

Official Answer: A

Explanation

Since this is an Inference question, let's look at each option and eliminate.

A. The correct answer. This can clearly be inferred from the first sentence of the stimulus
B. This may not necessarily be true on the basis of the information in the stimulus.
C. The argument clearly says this is not the case. As long there is demand for the product at that price, the manufacturer is doing no wrong in selling it at that price.
D. No such conclusion can be arrived at from the argument. If there is a high demand for the product, then it can be sold at a high price
E. Extreme option. The manufacturer may or may not fail but doesn't necessarily have to fail

14) A jewellery manufacturer produces rings in two metals – gold and platinum. The manufacturer has noted that, over the last three years, the gold rings have consistently outsold the platinum ones by a large margin, even though the designs available in both the metals are exactly the same. This has led the manufacturer to conclude that consumers prefer gold to platinum.

Which of the following, if true, most seriously weakens the argument?

(A) Over the last three years, diamond rings have outsold both gold and platinum ones

(B) Jewellery buyers give more importance to design than to the metal used

(C) Platinum is easier to maintain than is gold

(D) Platinum rings take longer to produce than do gold rings

(E) Gold rings cost considerably less than do platinum ones

Official Answer: E

Explanation

The argument concludes that just because gold rings sell more than platinum rings, customers prefer the metal gold to the metal platinum. But there can clearly be other reasons why customers prefer gold rings to platinum ones – maybe the gold rings are cheaper or have better designs or are easier to resell. Any such option can weaken the argument. (E) highlights the cost aspect and should be the correct answer

A. The argument is only concerned with gold and platinum rings. Diamond rings are outside the scope of the argument
B. This does not necessarily suggest that customers don't pay attention to the metal used or that gold rings have better designs than platinum ones. Maybe the second item on the customers' preference checklist, after the design, is the metal used.
C. So then platinum rings should be selling more, why are gold rings selling more?
D. How much time it takes to produce a ring in either metal is irrelevant
E. The correct answer

15) The country has recently been shaken by the increase in incidents of corruption amongst the political class and the bureaucracy. The solution clearly is to appoint an independent investigating body headed by a person of repute who can investigate such cases of corruption and punish those found guilty.

The conclusion above would be more reasonably drawn if which of the following were inserted into the argument as an additional premise?

(A) The appointment of the independent body is the only way to combat corruption

(B) The independent agency will itself not fall prey to corruption

(C) Corruption is not present outside the political class and the bureaucracy

(D) The punishment meted out by the investigating agency will not act as deterrent for people/agencies susceptible to corruption

(E) If not controlled immediately, the problem of corruption can spiral out of control

Official Answer: B

Explanation

The question is asking you to identify an additional premise that is not stated in the argument, which is the same as the assumption. So you basically need to identify the assumption in the argument. The assumption in the argument has to be the fact that the investigating agency or the person heading it will itself/himself not fall prey to corruption. (B) states this and is the correct answer.

A. This does not necessarily have to be the case. There could be other ways of fighting corruption but they are outside the scope of the argument
B. The correct answer. If you negate this the argument will fall apart
C. This may or may not be true but doesn't have to be true for our conclusion to be true
D. In fact the idea should be the opposite – that the punishment meted out would act as a deterrent for others
E. This is a general statement and not the assumption of the argument

16) Almost all arguments against the theory of evolution stem from the fact that it is very difficult to prove how a group of non living elements can combine together and give rise to life. However, just because something cannot be proved with certainty today doesn't mean that the possibility isn't there. Remember, there was a time when almost the whole world believed that the Earth was the centre of the universe until Galileo came by and proved otherwise.

The statements above, if true, best support which of the following assertions?

(A) At one point of time, Galileo was the only person who believed that the earth was not the centre of the universe

(B) A majority of scientists do not agree with the theory of evolution

(C) It is difficult to prove the theory of evolution with certainty

(D) When Galileo stated that the sun and not the earth was the centre of the universe, he was called insane by his compatriots

(E) Everything that at one time seems impossible will at some point in the future become possible

Official Answer: C

Explanation

Since this is an Inference question, let's look at each option and eliminate.

A. We can't say this for sure. There may have been more people who believed so but were scared of speaking up
B. We know for sure that some scientists do not agree with the theory of evolution. However, whether they are in majority or not is something we do not know.
C. The correct answer, this almost paraphrases the opening lines of the stimulus
D. While a lot of you may know that this is true, this cannot be inferred from the stimulus
E. Extreme generalization. May not be true for everything and the argument never suggests this anyway.

17) 30 years ago residents of Pandora County used to buy an average of 10 books every year. Today the residents of Pandora County buy an average of 3 books every year. Therefore it can be concluded that book sales in Pandora County must have fallen over these 30 years.

The argument above rests on which of the following assumptions?

(A) The residents of Pandora County used to have more free time 30 years ago than they do now

(B) The residents of Pandora County have many more activities that vie for their attention today than 30 years back

(C) The population of Pandora County hasn't increased significantly in the last 30 years

(D) The literacy rate hasn't significantly changed in Pandora County over the past 30 years

(E) Those residents of Pandora County who used to read 30 years ago have now not become too old to read

Official Answer: C

Explanation

The argument concludes that since the average number of books purchased per person in Pandora County has decreased over the past 30 years, the total book sales in Pandora County must have also decreased. But what if the population of Pandora County has increased several times in the past 30 years? So earlier if 100 people were buying 10 books each to give a total sale of 1000 books, today 500 people may be buying 3 books each to give a total sale of 1500 books.

So for the conclusion to be true the assumption has to be that the population of Pandora County hasn't increased significantly over the last 30 years. (C) states this and is the correct answer.

A. How much time each resident spends reading has no connection with how many books are sold.
B. This is irrelevant to the argument
C. The correct answer
D. While the literacy rate may seem relevant, this option may or may not be true but it doesn't have to be true for our conclusion to be true.
E. This is irrelevant to the argument

18) Which of the following most logically completes the argument below?

A new palm vein scanning technology is being developed by scientists that could be used with laptops or other tablet devices. This technology involves the use of a biometric sensor that can scan the unique pattern of veins in a person's palm to verify his identity. This technology could do away with the problem of remembering multiple passwords to access different websites. However the technology would require new biometric sensors to be built into computers but this should not be a hindrance in the success of the new technology, because____________________________.

(A) the new technology is bound to be extremely popular with computer users

(B) the biometric sensors do not cost a lot of money and are available in plentiful supply

(C) most people have forgotten one or more of their passwords at some point in their lives

(D) there is almost always a market for innovations such as these

(E) the biometric sensors can be easily and cost effectively built into computers

Official Answer: E

Explanation

Since the leading word is *because*, we need to strengthen the conclusion that the requirement of biometric sensors to be built into computers will not be a problem. (E) does this best and is the correct answer

A. The technology may be popular but if this technology is very expensive, then most people may not be able to afford it.
B. Even if the biometric sensors themselves are cheap, their installation in computers could be very expensive
C. This is an irrelevant fact
D. The market may not be there if these innovations become very expensive
E. The correct answer

19) Switzerland's national rail company has accused Apple of stealing the iconic look of its station clocks for Apple's new operating system. According to the rail company, both designs have a round clock face with black indicators except for the second hand, which is red.

Which of the following, if true, most seriously weakens the argument above?

(A) Apple has never been accused of copying by any other person or organization in the past

(B) Apple is know the world over for its unique product designs

(C) The designer who created the watch design for Apple's operating system has never visited Switzerland or any other European country for that matter

(D) All round face clocks across the globe are created out of the same design philosophy

(E) The Switzerland National Rail Company has itself been accused in the past of copying the platform design of a neighbouring country's railway platform

Official Answer: D

Explanation

The Swiss rail Company has sued Apple because of a similarity in the design of their respective clocks. (D) weakens this by suggesting that Apple may not have copied the design of the Swiss Rail Company. It's just that the source of design for the Swiss Rail Company and for Apple may have been the same.

A. Irrelevant, since if something hasn't happened till now does not mean it will never happen in the future.
B. But there is clear evidence of similarity between Apple's design and that of the Swiss Rail company
C. The designer may have seen the photo of the design in a magazine or somewhere else
D. The correct answer
E. This fact is irrelevant to the argument

20) Angel dusting is a process wherein an ingredient, which would be beneficial in a reasonable quantity, is instead added by manufacturers to their products in an insignificant quantity so that they can make the claim that their product contains that ingredient, and mislead the consumer into expecting that they will gain the benefit of that ingredient. For example, a cereal may claim it contains "10 essential vitamins and minerals", but the amounts of each may be only 1% or less of the Reference Daily Intake, providing virtually no benefit or nutrition.

If the above statements are true, which of the following could be an example of Angel dusting?

(A) A laptop that claims to have the longest battery backup, actually has a backup just 10% longer than is provided by its closest competitor

(B) A book that claims to cover all the concepts of Organic Chemistry actually provides just one example of each concept

(C) A vitamin capsule that claims to contain 23 vitamins and amino acids contains less than 3% of each

(D) A protein shake that claims to contain a magic ingredient that can make muscles grow faster, only contains 20% of this ingredient's daily recommended intake

(E) An apartment that claims to have used Italian marble for its flooring has used exactly one slab of Italian marble and the remaining ninety-nine slabs of regular marble.

Official Answer: E

Explanation:

(E) is the correct answer. If the advertising suggests that the use of Italian marble has been done in the entire apartment and in fact only one out of hundred tiles is made of Italian marble, then it is as good as not having Italian marble in the apartment at all.

A. This does not suggest that the laptop has a short battery back up
B. The book claims to cover all the concepts, which it apparently does; it never claims to provide several examples of every concept
C. Irrelevant. We have no idea whether 3% of these vitamins and amino acids is adequate or inadequate. Even if the 23 ingredients are equally divided each will comprise around 4% of the capsule, so 3% is not as low as it sounds. In any case we don't have any reference data
D. Again we don't have any reference data. It is possible that 20% of the magic ingredient coming from one source is a very good thing because the other sources contain less than 1% of the daily recommended intake of this ingredient
E. The correct answer. This option is the best of the lot because it gives you a reference figure of 99 tiles. If the apartment had five slabs of marble and one of them was Italian marble, then this may not necessarily be an example of Angel dusting, but the use of one tile out of ninety nine is definitely an example of Angel Dusting. This is the best option in our lot.

21) In the year 2000 olive oils made up just 40% of the liquid oils market, with standard oils taking 52% and speciality oils accounting for the remainder. But now, fuelled by health concerns and a general move towards premium products, the tables have turned. Today, the olive oil sector is worth some $104 million and alone accounts for an estimated 51% of the total market.

Which of the following conclusions can most properly be drawn from the information above?

(A) In 2000, the total worth of the olive oil sector was less than $104 million

(B) The total sales of the standard oils at present time are lower than their sales in 2000

(C) Olive oil is healthier than all other liquid oils available in the market

(D) The market share of the standard oils category today must have declined from what it was in 2000

(E) The total worth of the specialty oil category today is higher than what it was in 2000

Official Answer: D

Explanation

Since this is an Inference question, let's look at each option and eliminate.

A. This does not necessarily have to be the case. What if the total market for liquid oils has shrunk? Then even though olive oil could have a larger share of this market, in absolute terms its total worth may have gone down
B. Again this may not be the case if the total market for liquid oils has expanded significantly
C. Extreme option. There could be healthier oils than olive oil available in the market
D. The correct answer. In 2000 the market share of the standard oils category was 52% and currently the market share of olive oils is 51%. So then the market share of standard oils category currently cannot be more than 49%, which is lower than 52%.
E. This may not be the case if the overall market for liquid oils has shrunk

22) The Langova National park is a breeding ground for several migratory birds. The Spot-breasted Laughing Thrush, an extremely rare species of bird, has been sighted only in the Langova National park of late. The people who have sighted this bird in the park have claimed that it is possible to sight this bird only through the use of binoculars. Barry is visiting the Langova National Park next week and he will be carrying an extremely powerful pair of binoculars with him. Therefore, it is safe to conclude that, as long as Barry has his binoculars on him, he will most definitely manage to sight the Spot-breasted Laughing Thrush.

Which of the following indicates a flaw in the reasoning above?

(A) It fails to take into account the possibility of sighting the Spot-breasted Laughing Thrush at places other than the Langova National Park

(B) It mistakes a necessary condition for a sufficient condition

(C) It is based on a series of assumptions, rather than on facts

(D) It does not take into account the possibility that Barry could lose or damage his binoculars on way to the park

(E) It does not take into account the possibility that Barry may sight some other equally rare species of bird

Official Answer: B

Explanation

The argument states that the Spot-breasted Laughing Thrush cannot be sighted without the use of binoculars so the use of binoculars is a necessary condition for sighting the bird. However this does not mean that just because one has a pair of binoculars, he will be able to spot the bird. The argument never states that everyone with binoculars spots this bird but that everyone who spots the bird has binoculars. (B) states this point and is the correct answer.

A. The argument is only concerned with the chances of spotting the bird inside the Langova National Park
B. The correct answer
C. The argument is in fact based on facts – it is a fact that people have spotted the bird using binoculars
D. The argument clearly states that as long as *Barry has his binoculars on him* he will be able to spot the bird. If he loses or damages his binoculars, then this is outside the scope of the argument.
E. Other species of birds are outside the scope of the argument

23) Jim Rogers: It's very difficult for foreigners to do business in India because India doesn't like foreigners and keeps them away. The biggest proof of this is Walmart, which has many stores in China, but not a single fully-owned store in India, simply because India doesn't like overseas businessmen.

Which of the following is an assumption made in drawing the conclusion above?

(A) There is nothing that can make India like foreign businessmen

(B) The fact that Walmart has many stores in China proves that China loves foreigners

(C) The limited size of the Indian market hasn't stopped Walmart from entering India

(D) Any foreign company other than Walmart is also not present in India

(E) China's policies are probably more favourable towards foreigners than are India's policies

Official Answer: C

Explanation

The argument concludes that the reason Walmart does not have any stores in India is because India does not like foreigners. However there could be other reasons as well for Walmart not doing so. Thus in arriving at its conclusion, the argument assumes that there could be no other reason for Walmart not entering India, such as Walmart itself not wanting to enter India. (C) points out one such passive assumption in the argument and is the correct answer.

A. Irrelevant to the argument and not necessary for the argument to be true
B. Whether China loves foreigners is not our concern
C. The correct answer
D. The argument never talks about any other company so this cannot be an assumption in the argument
E. This may be an inference but is definitely not an assumption

24) Which of the following most logically completes the argument?

A recent experiment has revealed that a person stands the best chance of surviving a plane crash if he or she is sitting at the back of the aircraft. A Boeing 727 was crashed on purpose into the Sahara desert and various aspects of the impact were analysed. One of the findings of this experiment was that dummies placed at the back of the airplane suffered much less damage than the ones placed at the front. Thus, when travelling by airplanes, you would be much better off sitting at the back, assuming ________________.

(A) that all the seats at the back of the plane haven't already been booked

(B) that the plane will be flying over the Sahara desert

(C) that the plane is manufactured by Boeing and has been part of the test described in the stimulus

(D) that the plane does not crash on its tail

(E) that these results apply to aeroplane crashes in general, and not just to those of old 727s into sand.

Official Answer: E

Explanation

Since the leading word is assuming, we need to find the assumption in the argument. The argument obviously assumes that what holds true for the crash test will hold true for other plane crashes as well. (E) states this and is the correct answer.

A. This is irrelevant to the decision at hand. The idea is whether it makes sense to sit at the back, not whether one actually gets to sit there.
B. Irrelevant. It could be any other desert. The assumption has to be whether this would apply to non-desert locations as well
C. If the plane has already been part of the test i.e. it has already been crashed, it won't be flying again in the first place
D. While this may look logical, the argument does not mention anything about how the plane used in the experiment actually crashed – on its tail, its front, its belly, etc. So then we cannot necessarily assume this fact
E. The correct answer

25) According to some people, income tax should be done away with in the US since there are several other ways to collect taxes. A few countries in Europe have successfully abolished income taxes by raising other taxes such as sales tax. Of course this makes products more expensive but with the added amount of money you would receive on your paycheck, you will still be better off than you were paying income taxes.

Which of the following, if true, provides the most support for the argument above?

(A) The prices of products in European countries, when converted into US dollars at current rates are very similar to their prices in the United States

(B) The increase in prices of products because of the increased sales tax rate will not more than offset the benefit of not paying any income taxes

(C) The legislative body in the United States has stated that it will support the move to abolish income tax

(D) Apart from increasing sales tax, the government can also increase other special taxes such as those on petroleum products

(E) The government has enough funds in reserve currently to be able to absorb any shock because of lowered tax collection

Official Answer: B

Explanation

The argument concludes that the increase in the prices of products because of an increase in the sales tax rate will not adversely affect the consumers because their salaries will also increase due to the abolition of income tax. However, what if this increase in the prices of products was much more than the increase in people's salary? Then the situation will negatively impact the people. The argument obviously assumes this will not be the case. (B) states this and so strengthens the argument.

A. The situation in European countries has no bearing on the situation in the US
B. The correct answer
C. This is an additional point and not relevant to the reasoning provided in the argument
D. Other taxes are outside the purview of the argument
E. The question is not whether the government will be able to bear the shock of abolition of income tax but whether such a move will be beneficial for the people

26) I do not agree that wage disparity still exists between men and women. Almost all salaried individuals today are paid based on their qualification and experience and not their sex. It is only the lower labour class where the disparity still exists, but this is justified because there are certain tasks requiring physical strength, such as carrying heavy construction material, that can only be done by men.

If the above statements are true, which of the following is an example of a wage disparity on the basis of gender?

(A) A company pays its management trainees, most of whom are females and have just passed out from business schools, a lower salary than it pays to its senior partners, most of whom are males

(B) A male labourer who does not do any physically taxing work is paid a lower wage than a male labourer who does physically taxing work

(C) A female employee at a managerial level in a company gets a lower salary than a female employee who has joined the company as a trainee but whose uncle is a partner in the company

(D) A male labourer who does not do any physical work is paid a higher wage than a female labourer who does not do any physical work

(E) A male manager working for Company X gets paid a higher salary than does a female manager with similar experience working for Company Z

Official Answer: D

Explanation

The argument concludes that wage disparities on the basis of gender do not exist anymore. It also provides an explanation for an apparent disparity in the wages of male and female labourers. (D) weakens the argument by stating that even though the male and female workers are not doing any physical labour, the male is still being paid higher wages than the female.

A. The wage disparity is on the basis of experience or seniority and not gender. The gender is just a coincidence
B. The comparison between two male labourers is irrelevant to the argument about gender disparity
C. Again the comparison between two female employees is irrelevant to the argument about gender disparity
D. The correct answer
E. While this may look good initially, it may very well be the case that the two companies in question have different wage standards. You can only do a correct comparison if you compare employees working for the same company.

27) A study of 1000 American citizens has found that 70 per cent of them would not work for a company with bad reputation even if they were unemployed and that nearly 90 per cent of them would consider leaving their current jobs if they were offered another role with a company that had an excellent corporate reputation. Of those willing to work for a company with a bad reputation, the research found that, on average, it would take doubling an employee's salary for them to make such a jump.

If the statements above are true, which of the following conclusions is most strongly supported by them?

(A) At least 10% of the people in the survey would not mind working for a company with a bad reputation but would also consider leaving their current jobs to join another company with excellent corporate reputation

(B) The survey is representative of the worker pool across the United States

(C) At least 25% of the people in the survey would agree to do an unethical act if their salary was substantially increased

(D) For US workers, higher salary takes precedence over the reputation of the company they work for

(E) If a company in the US expects to attract the best talent, it must either have an excellent corporate reputation or be ready to pay high salaries

Official Answer: A

Explanation:

According to the stimulus, 300 of the 1000 people would be willing to work for a company with a bad reputation. Also 900 people would consider leaving their current jobs if they were offered a role with a company that had an excellent corporate reputation. Since the total number of people is only 1000, it has to be the case that (300-100) 200 people will be such that they would belong to both the above groups. (A) states this best and is the correct answer. Don't be confused by the fact that (A) mentions 10% and not 20% (200 out of 1000); notice that (A) uses the term *at least* 10% i.e. at least 100 people.

A. The correct answer
B. The argument only talks about the pool of 1000 people who were surveyed and does not conclude anything for workers across the United States
C. The argument never really describes what constitutes an unethical act
D. We cannot really conclude this for all workers in the United States
E. Extreme inference. There could be a third situation as well apart from these two.

28) One way in which companies can increase their productivity is by making use of telecommuting. Many office workers waste a lot of time in their cars or other modes of road transport every morning trying to reach office, and a lot of them spend their day attending video conferences and typing emails, activities which could easily be carried out from the comfort of their homes. So it makes sense for companies to encourage their employees to use telecommuting services and work from home rather than travel to the office every day

In order to evaluate the above argument, it would be useful to determine each of the following EXCEPT:

(A) Whether the cost of telecommuting will more than offset the increased productivity that comes about from its use

(B) Whether the day to day work of most companies involves physical interaction amongst their employees

(C) Whether a large part of the work of an average employee can be conducted using telecommuting services

(D) Whether the use of telecommuting service will lead to increased revenues for the companies adopting this service

(E) Whether the general traffic situation is likely to dramatically improve in the future

Official Answer: D

Explanation:

Let's look at each of the option and check whether it is relevant to the argument.

A. Relevant. If there is no cost benefit of telecommuting, then companies may not want to make use of it
B. Relevant. If employees' work requires physical interaction then telecommuting may not make sense
C. Relevant. If most of an employees' work entails coming to the office then it may not make sense to use telecommuting
D. Irrelevant. Even if the revenues remain the same, the cost could go down because of telecommuting, leading to increased profits from the same revenue base. So it does not matter whether the revenues go up or not
E. Relevant. If the traffic situation improves dramatically in the future, then it might take care of the problem associated with coming to work

29) Barney has noticed a unique trend in his college test results over the last two semesters. When Barney was in Semester 1 he studied for two hours every day and got a score of 80 on 100 in his final test. In semester 2, Barney studied for four hours every day, yet he only scored 60 on 100 in his final test.

Which of the following, if true, most helps to explain why Barney's grades are declining even though he is spending more time studying every day?

(A) Barney studies with more concentration now than he used to in semester 1

(B) Even though his grades have gone down, Barney has become much more knowledgeable now than he used to be earlier

(C) Barney's classmates also, on an average, scored higher in semester 1 than they did in semester 2

(D) Barney participated in several sporting activities in the first semester

(E) In Barney's college, the topics taught in semester 2 are considerably more difficult than those taught in semester 1

Official Answer: E

Explanation

The stimulus states that, even though Barney studies for more hours now than he used to earlier, his grades have fallen down. (E) provides one explanation for this by suggesting that the course may have become so difficult that the increased hours of studying are also not sufficient to cope up with it.

A. Then why are his grades going down?
B. The question at stake is not whether Barney has become more knowledgeable but why are his grades going down.
C. Still doesn't explain why this is the case with Barney
D. Yet he scored more, so then why have his grades fallen in the second semester
E. The correct answer

30) Researchers have found that one in five patients hospitalized for heart attack experiences a major depression. According to the cardiologists who conducted the research, the depressed patients are fifty five percent more likely than other heart attack patients to need hospital care for a heart problem again within a year and three times as likely to die from a future attack or other heart-related conditions.

If the statements above are true, which of the following must be true?

(A) If a person dies of a heart attack, there is a high probability that he may have been suffering from depression as well

(B) If a patient needs to be re-hospitalised for a heart related problem within a year of his earlier heart attack, it is very likely that he may be suffering from depression

(C) There are some similarities between symptoms of depression and symptoms of a heart attack in a patient

(D) Depressed people are more likely to die of a heart attack than are people who do not suffer from depression

(E) Suffering from a heart attack can lead to depression in some people

Official Answer: B

Explanation

Since this is an Inference question, let's look at each option and eliminate.

A. This may or may not be the case. The argument never states that there is a causal link between all depression and heart attack cases. It just states that those depression patients who have already had a heart attack have a high chance of suffering or dying from a heart ailment
B. The correct answer. This is definitely true because for such a patient there is a 55% chance that he may be suffering from depression
C. The argument never makes any mention of the symptoms of a heart attack or of depression
D. Same as A, there is no direct link between depression and heart attacks for regular people
E. While this may look good, the argument never states what is the reason for this depression – heart attack or something else.

31) The real estate market in Kayman city, which had so far been insulated from the weak demand for real estate in the rest of the country, is finally starting to feel the heat. According to a real estate advisory firm, the sales of residential property in Kayman city this year decreased by almost 25% from the same period last year.

Which of the following, if true, most strengthens the above argument?

(A) The sales of residential property in the rest of the country did not fall by more than 25% this year

(B) The sale of commercial property did not comprise the majority of real estate transactions in Kayman City this year

(C) A percentage decrease is the same as a decrease in the absolute number of sales of residential property in Kayman City this year

(D) The reduction in the sales of residential property in Kayman City is a recent phenomenon

(E) Most of the reduction in sales of residential property in Kayman City has come about because of the steep increase in interest rates charged by banks on home loans

Official Answer: B

Explanation

The argument concludes for the real estate market in Kayman City in general whereas it provides evidence only for residential property. Clearly the assumption is that the trend visible in the market for residential property will also apply to commercial and other types of property. (B) states this and is the correct answer because the assumption always strengthens the argument.

A. Even if the sales figure in the rest of the country was worse than the figure for Kayman City, it does not take away from the fact that Kayman city has also started to feel the heat of a slowing market
B. The correct answer
C. This again doesn't have to be assumed but is stated in the evidence itself. If the sales have fallen by 25% from last year's figure, there is no way the actual number of sales could have increased
D. The argument already states that this reduction has happened in the current year so this option basically repeats the evidence
E. The reason for the reduction in sales is not our concern

32) A recent survey of buyers of luxury cars in Beecham city has revealed that males who are between 40 and 50 years of age and who live in the Southern part of the city are more likely to buy these cars than is any other demographic group in the city. Maxpages is a magazine that contains articles primarily relevant to males in the age group of 40 to 50 years and is circulated only in the Southern part of Beecham city. Using the findings of this survey, Terence, who owns two luxury car showrooms in Beecham city, has decided to advertise in the Maxpages magazine.

Which of the following would it be most useful to know in determining whether Terence should advertise in the Maxpages magazine?

(A) What is the exact number of luxury cars that were sold in all of Beecham city in the last one year?

(B) What percent of the total car market is the luxury car market in Beecham city?

(C) Do women and children play a major role in determining which luxury car to buy?

(D) Is the luxury car market in Beecham city expected to grow over the next few years?

(E) Will it would be cheaper to advertise in some other magazine that is targeted at people of all age groups?

Official Answer: C

Explanation

The argument states that since most buyers of a particular product belong to a particular demographic group, it makes sense to advertise in a magazine that is targeted at that particular group. But what if the actual purchase decision was not taken by this group but by some other group such as women and children? Then it would make more sense to advertise in magazines targeted at women and children. Option (C) raises this point and is the correct answer.

A. This fact has no bearing on which magazine Terence should advertise in
B. This could have a bearing on deciding whether Terence should open a luxury car showroom at all anywhere in Beecham City. However that is not the question at hand.
C. The correct answer
D. Same as (B)
E. Irrelevant. The idea is to advertise in the magazine that is targeted at the prospective customer.

33) Which of the following best completes the passage below?

A study was recently conducted to determine whether power lines caused some kind of negative health effects. The researchers surveyed everyone living within 200 meters of high-voltage power lines over a 15-year period and looked for statistically significant increases in rates of over 1000 ailments. The study found that the incidence of childhood leukaemia was four times higher among those who lived closest to the power lines. However, this statistic by itself should not be a cause for alarm, because__________________________.

(A) child leukaemia can also be cause by other genetic factors

(B) another study has found that most of the children who suffer from child leukaemia stay far away from power lines

(C) the number of potential ailments, i.e. over 1000, was so large that it created a high probability that at least one ailment would exhibit statistically significant difference just by chance alone

(D) there was no significant correlation between the other 999 diseases and how close to power lines a person stayed

(E) child leukaemia, unlike leukaemia in adults, can be cured by medicines and therapy and is rarely fatal

Official Answer: C

Explanation:

Since the leading word into the blank is *because*, we need to strengthen the fact that the statistic given in the stimulus is not a cause for concern. (C) does this best by stating that the number of diseases that the study took into consideration was very large to be statistically significant. An analogy for this could be related to the stock markets, where if you track 1000 stocks for how the stock performed on the days on which you wore a black T-shirt, you will most likely find a correlation between some stocks performing well and the colour of your T-shirt. This cannot lead you to conclude that on the days you wear a black T-shirt the stocks of these companies will definitely perform well.

A. Our concern is proximity to power lines; we are not concerned with the other causes of leukaemia
B. But how do we explain the results of the study mentioned in the stimulus
C. The correct answer
D. Even if this is the case, we still need to explain the correlation between that one disease – leukaemia – and proximity of people to power lines
E. We are concerned with the cause of the disease and not its cure

34) The mayor of Newtown is up for re-election in a month's time and is extremely apprehensive of his chances. According to a recent survey conducted by a news channel in Hampstead, Newtown's most populous suburb, more than 80 percent of the respondents stated that they would not vote for the current mayor.

The mayor's apprehensions are based on which of the following assumptions?

(A) The people who were part of the survey will in no case change their mind.

(B) The opinion of the residents of Hampstead is a pretty accurate representation of the opinion of the residents of Newtown as a whole

(C) The mayor was recently involved in a corruption scandal that received a lot of negative publicity in the print media

(D) The mayor did not do enough to help the victims of the hurricane that struck Newtown last year

(E) In the last three elections for the post of the mayor in Newtown, the incumbent mayor has never been re-elected to office

Official Answer: B

Explanation

The use of the word *survey* in the stimulus should give you a hint that you need to look for an error of Representativeness in this question. The mayor's conclusion is based on the results of the survey but the survey was just conducted in Hampstead. What if the residents of Hampstead don't like the mayor for personal reasons? Then the residents of other localities might still vote for the mayor and the mayor could still win.

So, for the mayor to conclude that his chances of victory are not very good, he has to assume that the survey in question was representative of the entire population of Newtown. (B) states this best and is the correct answer.

A lot of the options (C, D, E) provide additional negative points about the mayor but these are irrelevant to the argument at hand, since the evidence in the argument is the survey of voters.

A. The mayor's conclusion is based on the results of the survey. What happens after the survey (whether people change their mind or not) is irrelevant.
B. The correct answer
C. This is not the reason why the mayor fears his chances
D. Same as (C)
E. Same as (C)

35) **The government has recently been severely criticized for its decision to block access to a few websites** on which malicious information and photographs were being posted. The government has responded to this criticism by stating that **while it believes in freedom of speech and expression, this was an emergency** and in such situations, you have to cut off the source of the problem.

In the argument given, the two portions in boldface play which of the following roles?

(A) The first describes a reaction to an action and the second describes an action taken in response to this reaction

(B) The first is a criticism that the argument disagrees with; the second is the point of view that the argument supports

(C) The first is the point of view of a group of people and the second attacks this point of view

(D) The first provides a counterpoint to the argument's conclusion; the second is that conclusion

(E) The first provides the criticism of an action and the second provides justification for the necessity of taking that action

Official Answer: E

Explanation

The argument describes a criticism of an act of the government and the government's justification of the same. The first bold part describes why the government has been criticized and the second provides the government's explanation of the same.

A. While the first part is correct, the second is not an action taken in response to this. In fact the second bold part is not an action at all, it's just an explanation
B. The argument never takes a stand on the issue so we don't know what it agrees or disagrees with.
C. The first is a criticism which cannot exactly be described as a point of view. Even if this were the case, the second just provides an explanation for this; it doesn't attack this
D. The stimulus does not have any conclusion as such
E. The correct answer

36) Customer reviews are becoming a fixture on retail and consumer brand websites, with over 70% of retailers planning to feature them by the end of the year. The accelerated adoption of customer reviews indicates a more enlightened approach to handling negative comments—that is, the acknowledgment that occasional negative reviews do not hurt sales.

Under which of the following conditions is the above strategy likely to backfire?

(A) The quality of the product in question is so poor that a customer is not likely to buy it in the first place

(B) There are frequent negative reviews for a product

(C) The 20% of the retailers who do not launch this feature decide to offer huge discounts on their products

(D) The customers of a product never come to know about the existence of this feature on the product website

(E) It costs retailers a considerable sum of money to implement this feature on their respective websites

Official Answer: B

Explanation

The argument states that the occasional negative review will not hurt sales but what if the negative reviews became more frequent. Then this strategy of encouraging customers to post reviews may backfire. (B) states this and is the correct answer.

A. If the customer doesn't buy the product then there will be no reviews – negative or positive
B. The correct answer
C. This may lead to a temporary reduction in sales for the remaining 80% of the retailers but is in no way connected to the strategy of encouraging customers to post product reviews
D. In this case the strategy may not work but it will definitely not backfire either. There will be at worst no effect.
E. This again has no connection with the strategy backfiring

37) A new study provides more support for the hypothesis that social support may strengthen people's immune system. This study actually found that social isolation and loneliness can impair the immune system. According to the findings of the study, lonely and socially-isolated first-year students mounted a weaker immune response to the flu shot than other students.

The argument is flawed primarily because

(A) it assumes that there can only be one cause for an effect

(B) it assumes that a necessary condition for an event is a sufficient condition for that event to occur

(C) it assumes that if a cause for an effect is removed, then the effect will in turn get reversed

(D) it mistakes a symptom for a cause

(E) it is based on unverified and subjective data

Official Answer: C

Explanation

Notice that the argument concludes that social support may strengthen the immune system. It concludes this on the basis of evidence that a lack of social support weakens the immune system. This however does not mean that providing support will strengthen the system, providing social support may not do anything. Hence (C) is the correct answer. Just because the cause is removed does not mean the effect will get reversed. It might remain unchanged.

A. Even if we take this causal relation to be true, there is a bigger flaw in the argument as described above
B. The argument is not concerned with sufficiency and necessity
C. The correct answer
D. The argument does no such thing
E. The data can clearly be verified and is not subjective at all

38) For the past two decades, Eton Coaching Institute has been the market leader in preparing students for the entrance test to medical schools in the country. While several new players have set up shop in the last few years, and have shown good results, it remains without doubt that if a student wishes to ace the medical school entrance test, his best chances are with Eton Coaching Institute.

The statements above, if true, best support which of the following assertions?

(A) There is something unique about the books provided by the Eton Coaching Institute that makes its students perform well in the medical school entrance test.

(B) If a student does not join the Eton Coaching Institute, he will most likely fail to clear the medical school entrance test.

(C) The teachers at Eton Coaching Institute are probably better than those at other institutes

(D) A student could clear the medical school entrance test, even if he hasn't prepared with the Eton Coaching Institute

(E) If a student has prepared with the Eton Coaching Institute, he will clear the medical school entrance test.

Official Answer: D

Explanation

Since this is an Inference Question, let's go through each option and eliminate.

A. Not necessarily. The books provided by Eton could very well be the same as those provided by other institutes; maybe it's the teachers at Eton who are unique
B. Extreme inference. The argument never states anything about the chances of a student clearing the medical entrance test. Maybe for other institutes the chances are 2% and for Eton the chances are 10% but even then 90 out of 100 students enrolled at Eton (and 98 of the 100 enrolled at other institutes) will not clear the test.
C. This is the opposite of A. It could very well be that the books at Eton are better and the teachers are not
D. The correct answer. The argument never states that a students' only chance of clearing the test is with Eton but that his best chances are with Eton. It is very much possible that a student enrols with some other institute (or doesn't enrol with any institute) and yet manages to clear the test
E. Same as (B)

39) It is extremely unlikely that the incumbent governor will be voted back to office in the coming elections. According to a recent survey of residents of the state, more than 80% expressed dissatisfaction with the governor's performance and almost 60% stated that they would vote for the governor's opponent.

Which of the following most strongly supports the argument?

(A) The views of most of the state's residents are in concordance with the views of the survey's respondents

(B) The governor has received a lot of bad publicity in the past owing to his involvement in a corruption scandal

(C) The survey covered only a small fraction of the state's populace

(D) The governor's opponent is very popular amongst the residents of the state

(E) The newspapers in the state are against the governor and favour his opponent instead

Official Answer: A

Explanation

The use of *survey* in the stimulus should give you a hint that you need to look for the issue of Representativeness in this question. The argument assumes that the views of the people in the survey are representative of those in the state as a whole. (A) states this best and is the correct answer.

A. The correct answer
B. Even though this is negative information, this does not have any connection with our evidence and so is irrelevant. For all you know the bad publicity could be for the wrong reasons which the public may have later realised and so now it might want to vote for the incumbent governor
C. This is the opposite of the correct answer. This raises doubts on the conclusion by suggesting that the evidence may not be representative in nature
D. The popularity of the governor's opponent is not the question in the argument
E. Same as (D), this is not the issue at hand

40) The decision to ban the use of hands free mobile phone headsets while driving is not justified. There is no doubt that mobile phone use while driving is distracting and dangerous. However, it is dangerous because drivers use their hands and eyes to operate the phone, when their full physical attention should be on the road. Hands-free technologies allow for mobile phone use without such distractions, and these options should remain legal.

Which of the following, if true, undermines the argument above?

(A) The functioning of the eyes and the hands is governed by the brain and there is considerable evidence to show that the use of mobile phones distracts the brain

(B) Most good quality hands free headsets are expensive which will discourage people from buying them

(C) Just because something is legal does not necessarily mean that it is safe

(D) There have been some incidents of road accidents involving drivers who were talking on the mobile phones using hands free technology while driving at the time of the accident

(E) There are other technologies available, such as the use of Bluetooth to connect one's mobile phone to the car's speaker system, that are much safer than the use of hands free devices

Official Answer: A

Explanation

The argument assumes that a driver will be able to use his hands and eyes unhindered if he uses a hands free headset. (A) weakens this by suggesting that this will not be the case because the use of mobile phone distracts the brain that will in turn distract the hands and eyes because the brain controls the functioning of these

A. The correct answer
B. The price is outside the scope of the argument. The question is whether the use of hands free headsets should be allowed at all
C. True but to weaken the argument we have to show how the use of hands free headsets is unsafe
D. The operative word here is *some*. There could be other reasons for these accidents as well, such as over-speeding or carelessness of the pedestrians.
E. The availability of other technologies is outside the scope. The question is whether the use of hands free headsets is safe or not

41) Researchers from a data analysis firm have found that the three most popular combinations -- 1234, 1111, and 0000 -- account for close to 20 per cent of all four-digit passwords. The researchers also found that every four-digit combination that starts with 19 ranks above the 80th percentile in popularity, with those in the upper 1900s coming in the highest. Also quite common are combinations in which the first two digits are between 01 and 12 and the last two are between 01 and 31.

If the statements above are true, which of the following must be true?

(A) The password 1922 will most likely be less popular than 1981

(B) The password 0123 will most probably be more common than 2331

(C) If a password was to be selected from a random list of 100 four digit passwords, there is a very high possibility that it will be 1234, 1111, or 0000

(D) One out of three four digit passwords will be 1234, 1111, or 0000

(E) Passwords starting with 19 are more popular than those starting with 21

Official Answer: A

Explanation

Since this is an inference question, let's look at each option and eliminate.

A. The correct answer. Since the numbers in the upper 1900s are more popular than the rest, 1981 has to be more popular than 1922
B. While you may think this is correct based on the last sentence of the argument, all that can be inferred from the last sentence is that the password 0123 will be a popular one. We cannot infer anything about how it would compare with the password 2331. There could be some other characteristic of 2331 that makes it more popular than 0123
C. Not necessarily. All that the argument states is that these three comprise close to 20% of all passwords, so there's only a 20% chance that the chosen password will be one of these three.
D. In fact one out of *five* four digit passwords will be one of the three mentioned since the chances are 20%
E. We know that passwords starting with 19 are popular but we don't know anything about passwords starting with 21

42) People in medieval times believed that lice were beneficial for their health, because there hardly used to be any lice on people who were unwell. The reasoning was that the people got sick because the lice left. The real reason however is that lice are extremely sensitive to body temperature. A small increase of body temperature, such as in a fever, will make the lice look for another host.

If the above statements are all true, then what was wrong with the reasoning of people in medieval times about the connection between lice and disease?

(A) They assumed that nothing else could lead to the disease except the lice

(B) They assumed that a correlation was actually a cause and effect relation

(C) They assumed that the sample size that they saw was representative of the entire population at that time

(D) They mistook the cause of something for its effect

(E) They assumed without warrant that a necessary condition is most definitely also going to be a sufficient one.

Official Answer: D

Explanation

The problem with the thinking of the early Europeans was that they assumed that the absence of lice was the cause and the disease was the effect whereas in fact disease was the cause and absence of lice was the effect. Thus they mistook the cause for the effect. (D) states this best and is the correct answer.

A. This still does not explain why the lice went away
B. The correlation is indeed a cause and effect relation; they just reversed the cause and the effect
C. The problem is never of representativeness
D. The correct answer
E. This argument is not one of necessary and sufficient conditions

43) Which of the following best completes the passage below?

Over the years, supporters of slavery have put forward several view-points to rationalize their belief. One such argument states that some people are meant to be slaves as part of the natural order of the universe, or as part of God's plan, and it is wrong to interfere with this by abolishing slavery. However, such an argument is flawed, because it fails to take into account the fact that ____________________.

(A) slavery is a cruel practice that does not find much favour with most people in this world

(B) just because something is part of God's plan does not mean it is the morally correct thing to do

(C) slavery is considered illegal in almost all the countries of the world

(D) there exist no certain criteria to distinguish between natural slaves and those who should not be enslaved

(E) just because something is meant to be does not mean that it has to be

Official Answer: D

Explanation

The sentence leading to the blank states that the argument is flawed so the blank basically has to highlight a flaw in the argument. Remember that the flaw is always linked to the assumption. Those who suggest that some men are meant to be slaves are obviously assuming that there is some way in which one can make out who these men are. The argument cannot be that just because somebody is a slave, he was meant to be a slave. It has to be the other way round that is somebody is a slave because he was meant to be a slave. Since there is no criteria for distinguishing between the two, the argument does not hold weight. (D) states this and is the correct answer.

A. This could be a negative aspect of slavery in general, but is definitely not a flaw with the argument
B. Again this may make sense logically, but isn't necessarily a flaw with the argument.
C. Same as (A) and (B)
D. The correct answer
E. Again logical but not a flaw

44) The list of the highest paying cities in the world is headed by cities in Switzerland. This serves to reaffirm the fact that people in Western European cities on average earn three times more than those in Eastern Europe. The fact that, in Switzerland, deductions from salary are relatively low, further widens the gap between net wage level earned there and in other countries, especially in the rest of Western Europe. The largest wage differences are in Asia, where the highest value (Tokyo) is twelve times higher than the lowest (Delhi).

Which of the following can properly be inferred from the statements above?

(A) The Swiss pay less money in taxes than do people in the rest of Western Europe

(B) Delhi is the poorest city in the Asian continent

(C) The wage difference between the richest and poorest cities of Eastern Europe is less than twelve times

(D) Switzerland is not situated in Western Europe

(E) Tokyo has more rich people than does Delhi

Official Answer: C

Explanation

Since this is an Inference question, let's analyze each option one by one.

A. We know that the Swiss have lower deductions from their salary but we don't necessarily know whether these are on account of taxes are some other heads
B. All that the stimulus tells us is that the average wage in Delhi is considerably lower than in Tokyo. We don't even know whether we have data for each city in the Asian continent so there is no way we can conclude that Delhi is the poorest city in the continent
C. The correct answer. The argument states that the difference between the highest and lowest wage rates is highest in Asia, so it has to be lower in all other places such as Eastern Europe
D. In fact the argument suggests that Switzerland is most likely situated in Western Europe.
E. Again this depends on the population of the two countries because the wage level in consideration is an average. So it's possible for Delhi to have more rich people than Tokyo but since Delhi also has many more relatively poorer people, this fact pulls the average wage down.

45) The perceived value of goods and services, rather than just their price, is becoming an increasingly prominent factor in the purchase decisions of modern consumers, a new report has indicated. Thus it can be concluded that consumers will be increasingly willing to spend extra on goods and services that are high-quality and durable.

For the above statements to be true, which of the following must be true?

(A) The price of a product plays no role in the making of purchase decisions by modern consumers

(B) There is a positive relation between the quality of a product and its durability

(C) The modern consumer is not likely to allow the quality of a product to determine his purchase decision

(D) The ideal way for manufacturers to charge more for their products is to increase the perceived value of their products in the minds of the modern consumer

(E) The durability of a product is in some way related to its perceived value in the minds of modern consumers

Official Answer: E

Explanation

Don't mistake this question for an Inference question; it is in fact an Assumption question. Notice the wording of the question stem; it states which of the options has to be true for the argument to be true i.e. the assumption.

The evidence states that customers would be willing to pay more for products that they perceive higher than the others. However the conclusion states that these customers would be willing to spend more on products that are high quality and durable. Thus the assumption has to be that high quality and durability are factors that increase the perception of a product in the customer's minds. (E) states this and is the correct answer.

A. Extreme option, the price may play a role but a smaller role than the perception of the product in the customer's mind.
B. No such connection can be arrived at on the basis of the argument
C. Opposite. In fact according to the last sentence of the argument, the quality of the product will be a deciding factor for the modern consumer
D. This could be an inference from the argument but is definitely not an assumption. If you are confused try negating this option. It will not make any difference to the argument.
E. The correct answer. If you negate this the argument falls apart

46) There has been a sudden spurt in the cases of suicide amongst teenagers in Tango city. On investigation, a public interest group discovered that all of these teenagers had been listening to songs by an alternative rock group, The Demons, at the time of committing suicide. When the public interest group listened to the songs by this rock group, they were aghast to hear lyrics that encouraged people to kill themselves. Accordingly, the city mayor has decided to ban the sale and download of all alternative rock band albums in Tango city with immediate effect.

Which of the following, if true, would most strongly support the position above?

(A) Songs with lyrics that encourage people to kill themselves can actually lead to people killing themselves

(B) Alternative rock groups other than The Demons also contain lyrics that encourage people to kill themselves

(C) It is not required to impose a similar ban on movies containing large scale violence and bloodshed

(D) If people don't listen to songs by The Demons, they will not kill themselves

(E) It is the responsibility of a mayor to protect the citizens of his city

Official Answer: B

Explanation

There is a disconnect between the evidence and the conclusion in this argument. The evidence only talks about The Demons but the conclusion generalizes this for all alternative rock groups. The assumption then clearly has to be that what applies to The Demons will also necessarily apply to other alternative rock groups. If this is not so then the argument will get weakened. (B) states that this is indeed the case and hence strengthens the argument.

A. Doesn't affect the connection between the Demons and other alternative rock groups
B. The correct answer
C. Movies are outside the scope of the argument
D. This is not relevant to the argument
E. What constitutes the mayor's responsibility is outside the scope of the argument.

47) The 17 countries of the Eurozone are all united by one currency - the euro, but that doesn't mean that there aren't price disparities in the continent. A sum of 20 Euros can buy you 35 cups of coffee in Portugal but only 7 cups of coffee in Greece. The same amount of money can get you 16 cartons of eggs in Malta, but only 7 cartons of eggs in Ireland.

Which of the following conclusions can most properly be drawn from the information above?

(A) On an average, a cup of coffee costs more in Portugal than in Greece

(B) A carton of eggs costs more in Malta than in Ireland

(C) Price disparities are an unusual phenomenon in the countries of the Eurozone

(D) The cost of a cup of coffee in Greece is the same as that of a carton of eggs in Ireland

(E) Portugal is a cheaper country to stay in than is Greece

Official Answer: D

Explanation

Since this is an Inference question, let's look at each option and eliminate

A. In fact a cup of coffee costs more in Greece than in Portugal
B. Again a carton of eggs costs more in Ireland than in Malta
C. There is nothing in the argument to suggest this
D. The correct answer. 20 Euros can buy you 7 cups of coffee in Greece, whereas the same amount of money can buy you 7 cartons of eggs in Ireland. Then the price of a cup of coffee in Greece and has to be the same as the price of a carton of eggs in Ireland.
E. No inferences can be made about how expensive a country is to stay in based on the information given in the argument

48) John, a stock broker, has a list of companies whose shares he recommends his clients to invest in. Over the past one year, the share price of 20 companies listed on the stock exchange has appreciated by 100% or more and 16 of these companies are part of John's list. Thus John claims that he is an expert at picking stocks and that more and more investors should park their funds with him to get the maximum return on their investment.

The answer to which of the following questions would be most important in determining whether an investor should park his funds with John?

(A) How many companies are there on John's list?

(B) Whether any other stock broker has also showed similar or better performance last year?

(C) What is the total number of companies listed on the stock exchange?

(D) Has John shown similar results in the previous years as well?

(E) Does John hire the services of someone else to identify stocks in which his clients should invest?

Official Answer: A

Explanation:

What if John has every company listed on the stock exchange on his list? Then even though the best performing companies will be part of John's list, the worst performing companies will also be part of his list. As against this, if John has 30 companies on his list, then his strike rate is very good. So to evaluate John's argument, we need to know how many companies he has on his list. (A) states this and is the best answer.

A. The correct answer
B. The performance of other stock brokers is outside the scope of the argument. We are only concerned with evaluating John's argument.
C. This fact is irrelevant to evaluating John's argument
D. John's previous performance is irrelevant in analysing his current performance.
E. Even if this is the case, it makes sense to invest with John as long as his argument can be justified

49) Which of the following best completes the passage below?

Measured globally, car use will go on rising, for as people in emerging markets get rich, they want the mobility and status that car-ownership offers. But in the rich world the decades-long link between rising incomes and car use has been severed and miles driven per person have been falling. This does not, however, warrant the conclusion that automobile manufacturers located in rich countries should brace themselves for tough times ahead, since ____________________.

(A) a reduction in car use does not necessarily indicate a reduction in car sales

(B) fears about smog and global warming have led many people in rich countries to prefer the use of public transport to that of private cars

(C) fuel prices are expected to increase further in the next few years

(D) there are several new car launches lined up in rich countries over the next couple of years

(E) relatively poorer countries will then probably generate even lower car sales

Official Answer: A

Explanation

We need to strengthen the conclusion that just because car use is going down in rich countries, the car sales will not necessarily go down in these countries. (A) does this best by pointing out that there is no real connection between car purchase and car use. I could purchase several cars but only use them to travel short distances.

A. The correct answer
B. This explains why the use of cars in rich countries may have gone down but that's not what we are supposed to do in this question
C. If fuel prices increase further people may not want to buy cars
D. Just because new cars are being launched does not mean these will find buyers
E. Irrelevant to the argument

50) For a broadband company, reliability and low cost are two prime issues. CBC Broadband Company has faced reliability issues over the past 6 months leading to a lot of its users shifting to other companies. To counter this, CBC has decided to offer very low subscription rates for new customers. This strategy will most likely prove successful in getting new customers to register for CBC's broadband service because CBC does not have any online public forum on which its customers can air their grievances, so the new customers will be unaware of the problems faced by CBC's existing customers.

Which of the following, if true, most seriously calls into question the explanation above?

(A) Any contact between CBCs existing customers and its target customers is extremely unlikely

(B) CBCs competitors have not faced any serious problems of reliability in the past six months

(C) There exist popular avenues apart from company owned online public forums on which customers unhappy with a company's service can air their grievances

(D) The government has passed strict laws that impose heavy penalties on companies that do not fulfil promises that they make to customers

(E) The reliability of CBCs broadband service is not expected to improve in the near future.

Official Answer: C

Explanation

The argument assumes that the only way new broadband users can come to know about CBC's poor service is through an online public forum run by CBC. To weaken this argument we need to point out that there could be other ways of finding this out as well. (C) states this and is the correct answer.

A. This strengthens the argument by suggesting that new customers may not come to know about the poor service provided by CBC
B. The position of CBC's competitors is irrelevant to our argument
C. The correct answer
D. This is extra information and not relevant to the evidence mentioned in the argument
E. But this won't make a difference if the new customers don't come to know about this fact

51) According to a recent survey conducted in the US, about 52.5 per cent of Americans are now owners of at least some type of a mobile phone device. Interestingly, the same survey also found that 66 per cent of Asian community in the US owns smart phones, making Asians the leading users of such devices in the country.

Which of the following conclusions can most properly be drawn from the information above?

(A) More Asians own mobile phones than Americans

(B) The Asian community owns the maximum number of mobile phones in the US

(C) Almost half the population of the US does not own smart phones

(D) Feature phones sell more in the US than do smart phones

(E) The Asian community in the US is very well off which is why they can afford the more expensive smart phones

Official Answer: C

Explanation

Note that the stimulus mentions two different terms – mobile phones and smart phones. The options will most likely try to confuse you between the two.

A. The evidence is only for Asians living in the US. From this we cannot make any conclusions about Asians in general
B. We know that the Asian community owns the maximum number of smart phones in the US, but we cannot necessarily conclude this for mobile phones is general
C. While you may dismiss this as another one of those trick options, this is in fact the correct answer. According to the argument 52.5 % of Americans own mobile phones, so then 47.5 % of Americans do not own mobile phones. Smart phones are also mobile phones so then it is correct to conclude that almost half the US population does not own smart phones
D. Since we don't have the actual number of either of these given to us, we cannot conclude this
E. This option explains why the Asian community can afford smart phones but is not an inference that can be made from the argument

52) The Georgetown Public School recommends that all its students take an active interest in playing chess. This is because, according to a recent medical study, those students who played chess on an average performed better in tests of general intelligence than those who did not play chess. Thus the school contends that playing chess will boost up the intelligence of its students.

Which of the following raises the most serious doubt about the conclusion above?

(A) Some students who perform well in tests of general intelligence do not play chess

(B) Intelligent students are the only ones who take an interest in playing chess

(C) A similar correlation has not been observed with regards to other sports such as baseball

(D) Some of the students who play chess perform poorly in subjects such as History

(E) There can be other ways in which a student could develop intelligence

Official Answer: B

Explanation

This is a classic case of correlation being confused with causation. Just because those students who play chess perform better in tests of intelligence does not necessarily imply that it is because of chess that these students have become intelligent. It could very well be that since these students are intelligent, they like to play chess, i.e. the causality could actually be the other way around. (B) points this out and is the correct answer.

A. The argument does not contend that playing chess is the only way to boost intelligence. There could be other ways as well. All the argument contends is that if a student plays chess then he or she will definitely become intelligent
B. The correct answer
C. Other sports are outside the scope of the argument
D. The argument restricts itself to tests of intelligence; there is nothing in the argument to suggest that all intelligent students will perform well in all subjects.
E. Other ways of developing intelligence are again outside the scope of the argument

53) George: The anti-drunk driving campaigns will not be successful. Some people are just immune to these campaigns and will drink and drive no matter what.

Shelly: Complete eradication of drunk driving is not the expected outcome. The goal is reduction.

Shelly responds to George by

(A) questioning the veracity of George's evidence

(B) suggesting that George's conclusion is based on incorrect assumptions

(C) partially agreeing with the main conclusion of George but disagreeing with his reasoning

(D) partially agreeing with George's point of view but suggesting that he has overlooked a beneficial effect

(E) contradicting George's reasoning and supplying an alternative reasoning

Official Answer: D

Explanation

Shelly suggests that George may have got the goal of the ad campaign wrong because the goal is not to eradicate drunk driving but to just reduce the cases of drunk driving. (D) states this best and is the correct answer.

A. Shelly never questions the authenticity of George's evidence. She in fact partly agrees with what he says; the only thing is that George concludes that the campaign will have no effect whereas Shelly concludes that it will have a beneficial effect
B. Shelly suggests no such thing about George's assumption; rather she suggests that George's conclusion may not be the intended conclusion of the campaign
C. Shelly does partially agree with George's conclusion but she never disagrees with his reasoning. She disagrees with George about whether the conclusion should actually be what George thinks it should be.
D. The correct answer
E. Shelly never contradicts George's reasoning but his conclusion, which also she partially agrees with

54) Despite all the science and massive budgets involved in modern sports, many sportsmen and women at all levels of sport swear by superstitions or elaborate event rituals to enhance their game. Irrational as it may sound, these superstitions clearly boost performance because almost all the top sportspersons across the world have some superstition or the other that they always adhere to.

Which of the following would most help evaluate the conclusion that superstition clearly helps sportspersons?

(A) Whether sportspersons who are not as successful also have superstitions

(B) Whether there is empirical proof that superstition boosts the performance of sportspersons

(C) Whether sportsperson who don't have any superstitions are also as successful as the ones who do

(D) Whether superstition helps boost an individual's self belief dramatically

(E) Whether all successful sportspersons across the world have some superstition

Official Answer: A

Explanation

The argument states that since every top sportsperson has some superstition or irrational belief, it must be true that these superstitions help them perform better (because they are all top sportspersons). But what if this was a mere correlation? What if all sportspersons in general have superstitions and not just these top sportspersons? Then there has to be some other explanation for the success of the top sportspersons. (A) points out this fact and is the correct answer.

A. The correct answer
B. Even if there is no empirical evidence, it is a fact that almost all leading sportspersons have a superstition.
C. This doesn't help negate the fact that those who succeed do so because of their superstitions. There may be other things that work for these sportspersons (who don't have superstitions) but for those who have superstitions, it could be the superstition itself that is responsible for their performance.
D. How superstition helps boost performance is outside the scope of the argument
E. The argument clearly states that *most* successful sportspersons have some superstition or the other so we don't need to know whether *all* successful sportspersons have some superstition or not.

55) The proposal requiring mutual fund companies to set aside a part of their fee for investor education is laudable but meaningless. The challenge actually lies in finding the right ways of educating investors and making them financially literate.

Which of the following, if true, most strongly supports the argument?

(A) People looking to invest in mutual funds currently lack the knowledge to make informed decisions

(B) Most mutual funds have accumulated large reserves of cash for investor education

(C) Investing in mutual funds is very different from investing in other financial instruments such as shares and debentures

(D) Financially literate customers, on the whole, provide more business to mutual fund companies than do financially ignorant ones

(E) Activities aimed at educating customers cost a lot of money and most mutual funds do not have the cash reserves to conduct such activities

Official Answer: B

Explanation

The argument concludes that it is of no use making insurance companies create a separate reserve for investor education because the real problem is not of lack of funds but of finding the right activities to educate customers. (B) strengthens this point by stating that insurance companies do have enough funds at their disposal so the problem has to be something else.

A. Even if this is true the reason for this could be that insurance companies do not have enough funds to spend on customer education. This could then weaken the argument by suggesting that insurance companies should indeed keep aside a part of their funds for customer education activities
B. The correct answer
C. Comparison of mutual funds with shares and debentures is irrelevant
D. Same as A
E. Same as A.

56) Food colouring can be a form of deception if it is used to make people think that a fruit is riper, fresher, or otherwise healthier than it really is. This is because bright colours give the subconscious impression of healthy, ripe fruit, full of antioxidants and phytochemicals. A variation of this strategy is to use packaging which obscures the true colour of the foods contained within, such as red mesh bags containing yellow oranges or grapefruit, which then appear to be a ripe orange or red.

Which of the following must be true on the basis of the statements above?

(A) When buying fruits one must check the actual colouring of the fruit and not of its packaging

(B) Food colouring is not always done with the intention of deceiving people

(C) Consumers should avoid purchasing fruits wrapped in mesh bags because this most likely suggests that the something is wrong with the fruit

(D) Bright colouring is an accurate method of judging the freshness of a fruit

(E) The presence of phytochemicals in a fruit will most likely dissuade consumers from buying that fruit

Official Answer: B

Explanation

Since this is an Inference question, let's look at each option and eliminate.

A. The argument never states this. In fact if the fruit has been coloured (in addition to being placed in some kind of packaging), then even looking at the colour of the actual fruit may not help
B. This can be inferred from the first sentence of the argument. Since this statement qualifies that food colouring can be deceptive only when used for a particular purpose, it can be concluded that food colouring may have other non-deceptive uses as well.
C. This may or may not be true but does not have to be true all the time
D. The argument in fact states the opposite
E. The argument states that fresh and ripe fruits are full of antioxidants and phytochemicals. Then there is no reason why a fruit with phytochemicals should dissuade customers from buying it

57) In an election, Candidate A received 70% of the total votes cast and Candidate B received the remaining 30% of the total votes cast. Thus Candidate A was declared the winner. Candidate B has disputed the results of the election saying that he is much more popular with the public than is Candidate A.

Which of the following, if true, most helps to explain why Candidate B lost the election, despite being more popular than Candidate A?

(A) The public has been opposed to some of the policies of candidate B

(B) Candidate A had recently been in the news because of his involvement in a corruption scandal

(C) Most of candidate B's supporters are factory workers whose work shift time clashes with the time of the day when election votes can be cast

(D) The voting was conducted in an extremely fair manner with no incidents of cheating reported from anywhere

(E) Candidate A spent more time canvassing for votes than did Candidate B

Official Answer: C

Explanation

The discrepancy in the argument is the fact that even though B is much more popular with the public, he only got 30% of the votes in the election while his rival got the remaining 70% of the votes despite being less popular. (C) explains this fact by pointing out one reason because of which Candidate B's supporters may not have been able to vote at all.

A. Yet, candidate B is more popular than candidate A, so why didn't he win
B. It is even more surprising how candidate A won then
C. The correct answer
D. This doesn't explain the discrepancy
E. But candidate B was more popular then why didn't he win

58) The airfares on almost all routes in the country have increased considerably in the past six months. In fact, on some routes, the fares have as much as doubled from what they were six months earlier. Since there has been no significant increase in the number of fliers in the country in the last six months, the media has blamed cartelization in the airline industry for this rapid increase in fares.

Which of the following, if true, undermines the argument above?

(A) The media is known to sensationalise events of public importance to gain more readership/viewership

(B) The airfares on some routes have actually fallen over the past six months

(C) Two of the six airline companies operating within the country have shut down operations in the last six months

(D) The price of aviation fuel increased drastically two years back and has remained at that level since then

(E) Other neighbouring countries have also seen similar rise in air fares but nobody has accused the airline companies in those countries of cartelization

Official Answer: C

Explanation

The conclusion is that airfares have gone up and the cause according to the argument is cartelization by airline companies. To weaken the argument, we need to provide another explanation for the same effect. (C) does this by suggesting that the reason for increase in airfares could be the fact that supply of seats in airplanes has gone down.

A. This is a general statement about the media and doesn't explain why the airfares have gone up.
B. This may be true but, according to the argument, in general the airfares have risen
C. The correct answer
D. Since the price of aviation fuel increased two years back, why have the airfares started increasing only in the past six months
E. What is true for other neighbouring countries is outside the scope of the argument

59) Clerical workers show more signs of stress during the work day than those in executive or higher positions. According to the findings of a study, employees on the lower levels of job hierarchy had higher blood pressure and increased heart rate in the mornings. They also had higher average levels of the stress hormone Cortisol throughout the day.

Each of the following is an assumption in the argument, EXCEPT:

(A) The study is representative of all employees in general

(B) High blood pressure cannot be caused by factors other than stress

(C) The hormone Cortisol does not itself cause stress

(D) Increased heart rate is a sign of stress

(E) The higher average salary and in general better lifestyle of the employees at the executive and higher positions to an extent insulates them from stress

Official Answer: E

Explanation

Since this is an EXCEPT question, we need to identify four assumptions in the argument and the fifth option will be the correct answer.

A. This has to be assumed because the conclusion is for all employees in general whereas the evidence is just the study. If the study were not representative of all employees, the argument would fall apart
B. This also has to be true for the argument to be true. If there could be other causes for high blood pressure, then we cannot necessarily conclude that just because certain employees in Britain have high blood pressure, they are under lots of stress
C. This has to be true for the argument to be true. The argument hinges on the fact that stress leads to Cortisol; if this causality were reversed the argument will fall apart
D. Same as (B)
E. The correct answer. This could be an inference from the argument or an explanation of the argument but is definitely not an assumption in the argument. Even if you negate this option, the argument will not fall apart

60) Which of the following best completes the passage below?

Those who suggest that higher education should be offered to all for free are wrong. The cost of providing higher education will most likely be more than its benefits. Many vocational jobs require apprenticeships and in-house training, rather than a college degree. In fact, this would likely further exacerbate the unemployment issue, since ___________________.

(A) there would be no way for government to recover the extra money that it has spent on providing free higher education

(B) there are more vocational jobs available currently than jobs requiring higher education

(C) there would simply be more qualified candidates vying for the same number of jobs

(D) the sole purpose of higher education should not be to get jobs

(E) the population of people in the working age group is expected to grow rapidly in the coming years

Official Answer: C

Explanation

Since the leading word into the blank is *since*, we need to strengthen the conclusion that offering higher education for free will worsen the problem of unemployment. (C) does this by suggesting that since many of the available jobs do not require a higher education degree (they instead require some vocational knowledge), those who receive higher education for free will only add to the number of people who were competing for the jobs available to that applicant pool. Thus the unemployment problem will get worsened because the number of people seeking jobs will increase but the number of jobs available will remain the same.

A. Even if the government cannot recover the extra money it has spent, there is no reason why the unemployment situation should get worsened
B. This is already stated in the argument but we need to explain how this fact will lead to a worsening of the unemployment situation
C. The correct answer
D. The argument is limited to getting jobs so this option is outside the scope of the argument
E. This fact has no connection with the worsening of the unemployment problem because of the availability of free higher education

61) Historical data for all the elections held in Gangnam City shows that all winning candidates have canvassed for at least 100 hours. In fact candidates who have canvassed for fewer than 100 hours have never ever won. Out of all the candidates contesting in the upcoming elections in Gangnam City, Candidate A has canvassed for 120 hours, Candidate B has canvassed for 150 hours, and Candidate C has canvassed for 90 hours.

If the statements above are true, which of the following conclusions is most strongly supported by them?

(A) Candidate B will most likely win the election

(B) Candidate C will most likely lose the election

(C) The winner of the election will either be Candidate A or Candidate B

(D) The results of an election cannot be solely dependent on how many hours a candidate canvasses for.

(E) If no other Candidate has canvassed for more than 150 hours, then Candidate B will win the election

Official Answer: C

Explanation

Since this is an Inference question, let's look at each option and eliminate.

A. The argument never states that the candidate who canvasses for the maximum number of hours wins the election. The argument only states that the winning candidates always canvass for more than 100 hours, so A could also win the election
B. The correct answer. This has to be true based on the information in the stimulus. Candidate C has canvassed for fewer than 100 hours and no one with such a track record has ever won the election, so it can be safely concluded that C will most likely lose the election. Note that *most likely* does not mean *definitely*
C. The argument never states that A, B and C are the only candidates standing for the election; there could be other candidates as well who could have canvassed for more than 100 hours
D. This can be a logical opinion but cannot be inferred from the information in the stimulus
E. Again the stimulus never states that the candidate who canvasses for the maximum number of hours will win the election, so this inference need not be true.

62) A stain-removing agent currently available in City X can remove the most stubborn of stains from clothes but is not very popular because it leaves behind a foul smell in clothes. It takes around ten days for the smell to completely go away from the clothes. Another stain-removing agent has just been launched in City X which is as effective at cleaning stains as the older one. An advantage of the new stain-removing agent is that its smell starts to go away from the clothes in two days itself. Thus this new agent should easily be able to outsell the older one.

Which of the following pieces of information would be most helpful in evaluating the above argument?

(A) the rate of growth or decline in sales of stain-removing agents in city X

(B) the total number of stain removing agents sold last year in city X

(C) the per capita income of people residing in city X

(D) the amount of time it takes for the smell of the new stain-removing agent to completely go away from the clothes.

(E) a comparison of the smell of the new stain removing agent with that of similar agents available in other cities

Official Answer: D

Explanation

The author suggests that the new stain-removing agent will outsell the older one, but it takes no account of the fact that there's a disparity in the information given. The smell of the new agent starts to wear off in two days, but we need to know how long it takes for the smell to wear off completely. Only then would we be able to compare the new and the old agents. (D) provides this information and is therefore the correct answer.

A, B, and C present irrelevant issues. Neither of these pieces of information helps us to differentiate between the two stain-removing agents.

E - We are just comparing the two agents available in city X. A comparison with cleaning agents available in other cities has no bearing on the argument.

63) While cooking pasta, most Italian chefs add some cooking oil. The reason for this is not difficult to ascertain. Oil by nature is a greasy substance so the use of cooking oil prevents the pasta from sticking to the utensil it's being cooked in.

Which of the following, if true, most seriously calls into question the explanation above?

(A) The oil used most often by Italian chefs in cooking is olive oil, which has a neutral taste

(B) While it is being cooked, the pasta never comes in contact with the oil

(C) There are some Italian chefs who do not use cooking oil while cooking pasta

(D) If added in large quantities, the cooking oil can spoil the taste of the pasta

(E) To provide added taste is not the reason why cooking oil is added to pasta while it is being cooked

Official Answer: B

Explanation

There could be two ways of weakening the argument – either show some other benefit of adding oil or show that the intended benefit mentioned in the argument could not have been the reason for adding oil. (B) does this by stating that since the pasta never comes in contact with the oil, the purpose of adding oil could not be to prevent the pasta from sticking to the utensil.

A. This discounts the possibility that taste could be a reason for adding oil, so then the reason could still be to prevent the pasta from sticking to the utensil.
B. The correct answer
C. The question is why do the chefs who use cooking oil while cooking pasta do so
D. This does not explain the need for adding cooking oil
E. Again this option does not discount the possibility of the chefs adding olive oil to prevent the pasta from sticking to the utensil

64) A survey recently conducted at the Global Business School has thrown up two interesting findings.

Finding 1: In the last ten years, students attending Professor James' Economics classes were more likely to score in the top 10% of the class than were other students

Finding 2: In the last ten years, most of the students who scored in the top 10% of the class did not take classes from Professor James.

If the statements above are true, which of the following must be true?

(A) The quality of classes conducted by Professor James has probably decreased

(B) The number of students not taking classes from Professor James has increased over the last ten years

(C) There must be some factor other than attending Professor James' classes that can also make a student perform well in the subject

(D) The overall quality of the students who have joined Global Business School in the last ten years has increased

(E) Professor James needs to change his teaching methods if he wants more students to attend his classes

Official Answer: C

Explanation

This is an inference question. Because of the wording of the two findings it may appear that they are contradictory in nature but this does not have to be so because finding 1 only talks about the likelihood of a student doing well. It never states that students attending Professor James' Economics classes were the only ones scoring in the top 10% of the class. So there could be other students as well who were scoring in the top 10% of the class and who had not taken classes from Professor James. Thus (C) can clearly be inferred from this as there must have been some other reason (other than Professor James' classes) for the excellent performance of these other students.

A. From the information in the argument, no inference can be made about the quality of classes
B. Again this may or may not have been the case but does not necessarily have to be the case
C. The correct answer
D. It is possible that the quality has remained constant or has even decreased in that the students outside the top 10% are probably doing much better than were earlier students.
E. No such inference can be arrived at from the information in the stimulus

65) Cyber security experts have warned that accessing the internet through mobile phones is much more dangerous than accessing the internet through a regular computer. A computer system has more resources and more storage, and you can use security software to protect it. However, this is not the case with mobile phones, which have limited storage and, therefore, limited capacity for security software.

If the statements above are true, which of the following is the best way to make mobile phones more secure?

(A) Launch new security software with enhanced features that can provide better protection to mobile phones

(B) Avoid browsing the internet through mobile phones as much as possible

(C) Use calling software such as Skype that allows people to make calls from a computer itself

(D) Not use mobile phone internet to carry out confidential activities such as internet banking

(E) Increase the storage capacity of mobile phones

Official Answer: E

Explanation

Note that the stimulus clearly states that the reason why mobile phones are more vulnerable than regular computers is not because of lack of security software for mobile phones but because mobile phones do not have enough storage for this security software. So to make mobile phones more secure, the storage capacity of mobile phones needs to be increased. (E) states this best and is the correct answer.

A. This won't serve the purpose if the new software cannot be loaded on to the phone because of the phone's limited storage capacity
B. This is a prevention method and does not make the phone more secure
C. Same as (B)
D. Same as (B)
E. The correct answer

66) The apex banking regulator in the country has stated that banks are favouring profits over customer welfare. This is because banks are not passing on the benefit of cut in policy rates to the borrowers. The regulator regretted that the lending rates of banks have not come down in tandem with reduction in the liquidity reserve ratio rate; rather the rates have gone up.

Which of the following, if true, is most damaging to the position taken by the apex banking regulator?

(A) Banks are in essence businesses so their primary motive should be to make profits

(B) The costs of running a bank have gone up considerably in recent times

(C) Many banks still invest a considerable amount of money in improving the banking experience of their customers

(D) The sales of several high value products such as automobiles and homes have gone down because of the high interest rate charged on loans by banks

(E) Even publicly owned banks have not passed on the benefit of lower liquidity reserve ratio rates to their customers

Official Answer: B

Explanation

The argument assumes that the only reason banks have not reduced lending rates is because they are trying to make more profits. But what if the cost of operation of the banks has gone up which is why they are not passing on these benefits to the end customer? (B) states this and is the correct answer.

A. This in fact strengthens the position taken by the apex banking regulator
B. The correct answer
C. This is a separate point and has no connection with the cause and effect link mentioned in the argument
D. This is an irrelevant fact
E. This again doesn't weaken the argument

67) David Spiegel stunned the world in 1989 when he revealed that certain therapy groups may help breast cancer patients live longer. These groups also seem to help them live better. So if you suffer from breast cancer there is a good chance that you can improve your life, and maybe even extend it, by joining a professionally led support/therapy group that uses Spiegel's "supportive-expressive" model.

If the statements above are true, which of the following conclusions is most strongly supported by them?

(A) It would be a good idea for cancer patients to be part of some support or therapy group

(B) Being part of a support/therapy group increases a breast cancer patients desire to get better

(C) One way of curing breast cancer is to make the patient join a support/therapy group

(D) Being part of a support/therapy group can have beneficial effects for certain groups of people

(E) Doctors recommend joining support/therapy groups as a means to alleviate the discomfort caused by breast cancer

Official Answer: D

Explanation

Since this is an Inference question, let's look at each option and eliminate

A. The argument is only about breast cancer patients so we can't make inferences about cancer patients in general
B. We know that being a part of a support group is beneficial for a breast cancer patient. However we don't know whether this is because being part of such groups increases the patient's desire to get better or because of some other reason
C. The argument never states that being part of a support group can cure breast cancer
D. The correct answer. This has to be true based on the information in the stimulus.
E. The argument never mentions anything about doctors so we can't infer this option

68) Most people erroneously believe that airplanes are dangerous modes of transport. Statistics clearly reveal that more people are killed every year in road accidents than in air crashes. So travelling by airplanes is in fact safer than travelling by a car or a bus.

Which of the following, if true, most strongly supports the above explanation?

(A) Airlines across the globe spend significant amounts of money every year on adding new safety features to their airplanes

(B) There is no country in the world in which the number of people killed in air crashes exceeds the number of people killed in road accidents

(C) In a recently conducted survey by an independent agency, a majority of the respondents stated that they felt safer while travelling by air than while travelling by road

(D) The number of people who travel by airplanes every year is roughly equal to the number of people who travel by road.

(E) The technology used in modern aircrafts is much more sophisticated than that used in most forms of road transport.

Official Answer: D

Explanation

The argument states that in absolute terms, more people are killed in road accidents every year than in airplane crashes. So the argument concludes that travelling by air is safer than travelling by road. However this can only be the case if the number of people travelling by airplanes was the same as the number of people travelling by road. (D) states this and is the correct answer

For example say 500 people die in plane crashes every year and 10000 people in road accidents. But what if only 1000 people travel by planes every year while 100000 travel by road. Then 50% of the people travelling by air die every year as against 10% of those travelling by road.

A. Just because airlines spend a certain amount of money on safety does not necessarily mean that they are safer than road transport
B. This may very well be true but can only be judged in light of how many people travel by airlines and by road every year
C. The perception of travellers is extra information. We need to strengthen the connection between the evidence provided in the argument and its conclusion
D. The correct answer
E. Sophisticated technology does not necessarily make airplanes safer than road transport

69) The government is aiming to roll out an ambitious project of providing free medicines to its citizens at public health facilities across the country. Once the scheme is launched, the government will provide free generic medicines to all patients coming to public health facilities. Opponents of the project have criticized it, stating that since the plan covers only generic medicines, most of the citizens will be outside its purview.

Which of the following, if true, would most weaken the criticism made above of the Health Ministry's strategy?

(A) The Health Ministry has made suitable arrangements to ensure that there is no shortage of generic drugs once the new scheme is rolled out

(B) A survey of public health facilities across the country has revealed that more than half of the prescribed medicines at these facilities comprise generic medicines

(C) Most of the country's citizens prefer branded medicines to generic ones

(D) The middle and lower income groups, which comprise a large chunk of the country's population, still frequent public health facilities to resolve their health issues

(E) The cost of running this scheme will eventually have to be borne by the citizens in the form of increased taxes

Official Answer: B

Explanation

The question requires you to weaken the criticism of the argument i.e. you need to weaken the argument of the opponents. In arriving at their conclusion, the opponents have obviously assumed that most of the patients are currently prescribed non-generic drugs. (B) weakens this by stating the opposite, and is the correct answer.

A. If most of the people are prescribed non-generic drugs, then it won't matter if the generic drugs are readily available
B. The correct answer
C. The preference of the citizens is irrelevant. If they are prescribed generic medicines they will obviously go for these
D. This is irrelevant because it makes no mention of generic and non generic drugs
E. The cost is not really our concern in this argument

70) Jimmy's colleagues at work have noted that the days on which he comes to office by his car, he is in a very good mood and the days on which he comes to office by his bike he is in a grumpy mood. When Jimmy is in a grumpy mood his efficiency falls by almost fifty percent. Jimmy is currently working on a very important project that requires him to work at full efficiency. Therefore, his colleagues have suggested that Jimmy drive to work every day until the project is complete.

Which of the following would it be most useful to determine in order to evaluate the argument?

(A) Whether there is some other way using which Jimmy's efficiency can be increased

(B) Whether being in a good mood makes Jimmy want to drive to work

(C) Whether the bike is actually the reason for Jimmy's bad mood

(D) Whether Jimmy is unhappy with his working conditions

(E) Whether some other staff member can take Jimmy's place on the current project

Official Answer: B

Explanation

The argument concludes that a mere correlation between coming to office by bike and being in a grumpy mood is actually a cause and effect relation. It also assumes that the bike is the cause and the mood is the effect and not vice versa. (B) points out this second point. If being in a good mood makes Jimmy want to drive to work, then it's not because he drives to work that Jimmy is in a good mood. So then, just by making Jimmy drive to work, it cannot be ensured that he will be in a good mood.

A. Irrelevant. We are only concerned about whether Jimmy's efficiency can be increased by driving to work.
B. The correct answer
C. This appears to be saying the same thing as Option (B) but is in fact a trap. Even if the bike is not the reason for Jimmy's bad mood, it holds true that whenever he drives to work he is in a good mood. Since this is the aspect we are concerned with, it doesn't matter what causes Jimmy's bad mood
D. Still doesn't take away from the fact that whenever Jimmy drives to work he is in a good mood. Why is this so?
E. Out of scope. Our brief is to evaluate one particular strategy, not to suggest alternative strategies.

71) There should be a ban on television commercials for prescription drugs. These commercials put preconceived notions in people's heads and make them ask for a drug from their doctor whose side effects they are not aware of. If a person needed that drug their doctor would have already known to prescribe it for him.

If the statements above are true, which of the following must be true?

(A) Most people who visit a doctor are already aware what drug the doctor will most likely prescribe to them

(B) Television commercials for prescription drugs don't have an educational aspect to them in that they don't educate the consumers about the use of various drugs

(C) Pharmaceutical companies try to sell harmful drugs to consumers by using deceptive advertising

(D) At least some people ask doctors to recommend to them medicines whose advertisement they have seen on television

(E) Doctors themselves at times use the advertisements for prescription drugs as a source of information to recommend medicines to their patients

Official Answer: D

Explanation

Since this is an inference question, let's look at each option and eliminate

A. The people are already aware of what drug they want their doctor to recommend and not of what drug their doctor might actually recommend
B. Nothing can be judged about the educational aspect of television commercials for prescription drugs from the stimulus
C. There is nothing in the argument to suggest arriving at such an extreme and generalized inference
D. The correct answer, this is the point of the entire argument
E. This may be the case but cannot be inferred based on the information in the stimulus

72) It is interesting to note that, of the ten different brands of digital cameras available in the market, the one that sells the most is the second most expensive of the lot. This camera also offers the best picture quality of all the digital cameras available in the market. Clearly the price of the camera plays no role in the customer purchase decision; it is the picture quality of the camera that matters to customers.

Which of the following, if true, would most seriously weaken the argument above?

(A) Between two similarly equipped digital cameras, most customers will prefer the lower priced one

(B) There is a direct correlation between the price of a camera and its picture quality

(C) Some customers only purchase the cheapest available digital camera, irrespective of its picture quality

(D) The second largest selling brand of digital camera, which is also the third most expensive in the market, offers poor picture quality

(E) Digital cameras are usually purchased by affluent customers for whom the price of the camera isn't a big consideration

Official Answer: A

Explanation

The argument arrives at an extreme conclusion. Just because price is not the main determinant of which digital camera to buy does not mean that price plays no role in the customer purchase decision, when it comes to digital cameras. (A) correctly highlights this fact by pointing out that while picture quality may be the number one consideration on customer's list of preferences, price also matters because between two similarly equipped digital cameras, most customers prefer the lower priced one.

A. The correct answer
B. This may be true but it does not weaken the argument
C. The use of *some* means that this cannot be the answer. Some customers prefer the cheapest available camera and some don't; this fact does not tell us anything about most customers
D. While this strengthens the fact that picture quality is not the only determinant of which digital camera to buy, this option does not weaken the fact that price plays no role in making this choice because this camera is still the third most expensive in the market, so customers couldn't possibly be buying it because of its low price
E. This again does not weaken the argument. It just explains why price doesn't play a big role in deciding which digital camera to purchase, but our agenda is to weaken this conclusion itself

73) Telecom subscriber: It seems that all the telecom companies in our country are working in an absolutely unprofessional manner. The online consumer complaint forum is full of negative comments about all these companies, irrespective of the brand, while there are hardly any positive comments.

Telecom company representative: But this is because the people who are happy with our service don't have any incentive to post comments.

The telecom company representative responds to the telecom subscriber's complaint by

(A) raising doubts about the source of the customer's evidence

(B) pointing out that the customer has ignored the positive reviews that telecom companies get

(C) highlighting that the evidence in question is not representative of the entire population

(D) agreeing with the subscriber's conclusion but contradicting his use of evidence

(E) providing evidence that raises doubts over the claims made by the telecom subscriber

Official Answer: C

Explanation

The telecom company representative basically states that the data the subscriber is referring to is self selecting that is these people have chosen to post their reviews and the only ones who have the motivation or incentive to do so are people who are dissatisfied with the services. Thus the data may not be representative of all users of telecom services. (C) states this and is the correct answer.

A. The company representative never doubts the customer's evidence, he only insists that it would be wrong to arrive at a particular conclusion by using this evidence
B. The company representative never does this
C. The correct answer
D. The company representative in fact does the opposite – he agrees with the subscriber's evidence but disagrees with his conclusion
E. The telecom representative does not provide any evidence

74) In a recent study of people afflicted by the Babblers syndrome an interesting fact was noted. The people suffering from this syndrome consumed dairy products in much larger quantities than people who were not suffering from this syndrome. Thus the study concluded that to reduce the chances of getting afflicted with Babblers syndrome, one should completely avoid the consumption of dairy products or consume them in moderate quantities at best.

The study's conclusion is based on which of the following assumptions?

(A) Excessive consumption of dairy products can have a negative impact on the health of people

(B) Babblers syndrome is a dangerous disease

(C) The effects of Babblers syndrome do not include excessive desire to consume dairy products

(D) Cutting down on dairy products will ensure that one does not contract Babblers syndrome

(E) Nothing else can lead to Babblers syndrome except the consumption of dairy products

Official Answer: C

Explanation

The study has found that two those who suffer from Babbler' syndrome also consume dairy products in large quantities. From this can we conclude that dairy products are the cause of Babbler's syndrome? There are two other possibilities – either something else is the cause of Babbler's syndrome or dairy products are the effect of Babbler's syndrome.

The argument's conclusion obviously assumes that neither of these possibilities will be true. (C) states one of these possibilities and hence is the correct answer.

A. We are only concerned about the connection between dairy products and Babbler's syndrome. Other health problems are outside the scope of the argument.
B. Irrelevant to our argument
C. The correct answer
D. The argument never concludes that the only way to contract Babbler's syndrome is by the consumption of dairy products. There could be other ways as well. Our point is to show that consumption of dairy products will definitely lead to a person contracting Babbler's syndrome.
E. Same as (D)

75) Which of the following most logically completes the argument?

It is now known that to get the maximum out of a car engine one can do two things - use high octane fuel, which contains additives that extend the life and efficiency of the engine, or get the engine flushed at regular intervals, which removes all harmful substances from the engine. It has been shown by several studies that the use of high octane fuel is up to three times more effective in extending the life of the car engine than is the use of engine flushing. This does not, however, mean that engine flushing can play no role in extending the life of a car engine, because _______________.

(A) some studies have shown that using high octane fuel can lead to problems with a car's exhaust system

(B) high octane fuel costs much more than regular fuel and this cost is expected to increase even further over the next few years

(C) many car mechanics recommend the use of engine flushing over the use of high octane fuels

(D) the benefits of using high octane fuel are independent of the benefits of engine flushing.

(E) engine flushing, when not done by expert mechanics, can cause permanent damage to the engine of a car

Official Answer: D

Explanation

The leading word *because* should tell you that you need to look at this question as a strengthen question. The conclusion is the last sentence of the argument i.e. it is incorrect to say that engine flushing can play no role in extending the life of a car engine. (D) strengthens this point by pointing out that the benefits of engine flushing and of using fuel with additives don't overlap, so if both are used together then the benefits could be higher than by using either of them alone.

A. For all you know there could be problems associated with the use of engine flushing as well
B. People might still be willing to pay this higher price for the sake of their car engines
C. The word *many* cannot really give the answer because many mechanics recommend and many don't recommend
D. The correct answer
E. This in fact weakens the argument by stating a negative aspect of engine flushing

76) The recent proposal by the government to introduce new conditions in the labour laws is a big setback to the IT industry in the US, especially at a time when it was expecting simplification of the currently applicable conditions. One of the proposed conditions, for instance, is that employers will have to disclose the names and locations of the clients hiring their workers, which will put them in automatic violation of non-disclosure agreements that are the norm in any contract.

Which of the following conclusions can most properly be drawn from the information above?

(A) The non-disclosure agreement bars IT companies from revealing the names of their employees working with different clients in the US

(B) If the proposed conditions come into effect, IT companies will not be able to carry on their operations in the US without violating client non-disclosure agreements

(C) The US government's actions will lead to reduced profitability of IT companies operating in the US

(D) The US government's actions with regards to changes in the country's labour laws did not exactly come as a surprise for most IT companies

(E) The IT industry will most likely curtail operations in the US if the US government does not take back its newly imposed conditions

Official Answer: B

Explanation

Since this is an inference question, let's look at each option and eliminate.

A. This is a trap option. The non disclosure agreement does not bar IT companies from revealing the names of their employees but those of their clients
B. This has to be true based on the information in the stimulus
C. The argument makes no mention of profits or sales so we cannot make any inferences about this
D. Opposite. The stimulus states that the IT companies had actually been expecting a favourable government policy
E. This may or may not be true. The IT companies could find some other way around the problem

77) **Existing optical lenses are not thin or flat enough to remove distortions,** such as spherical aberration and astigmatism, which prevent the creation of a sharp image. Correction of those distortions requires complex solutions, such as multiple lenses that increase weight and take up space. To overcome these challenges, scientists have developed a new superthin, flat lens. **The surface of this lens is patterned with tiny metallic stripes which bend light differently as one moves away from the centre,** causing the beam to sharply focus without distorting the images.

In the argument given, the two portions in boldface play which of the following roles?

(A) The first states a problem with existing optical lenses and the second states the solution for this problem that has been developed by scientists

(B) The first is the main conclusion of the argument and the second provides support for this main conclusion

(C) The first is evidence the accuracy of which is questioned later in the argument; the second is a conclusion that the argument supports

(D) The first mentions a problem with existing optical lenses and the second describes the structure of a new type of lens that can solve that problem

(E) The first is a problem associated with one type of optical lens; the second advocates the use of an alternative lens

Official Answer: D

Explanation

The argument basically states that there is a problem associated with currently available optical lenses and that scientists have developed a new type of lens that can resolve this problem. The first bold part describes the problem and the second bold part describes the structure of the new optical lens and how it works.

A. While this option looks good, notice that the second bold part does not actually state the solution to this problem; it just provides a description of the new optical lens.
B. The first and second bold part are in fact stating opposite things so one cannot be providing support for the other
C. The accuracy of the first bold part is never at question in the argument. The second is not really a conclusion
D. The correct answer
E. The first bold part is correct but the second bold part incorrectly uses the term 'advocate'. The argument never advocates anything

78) Ever since the new Marketing Head joined Crackwell Corporation, its profits have increased steadily. In fact, over the past three years that the Marketing Head has been with Crackwell, the company's profits have grown by almost 35% every year, a figure that used to hover around the 10% mark earlier. Pleased by this fact, the Board of Crackwell Corporation has decided to reward the Marketing Head with stock options in the company.

Which of the following, if true, casts the most serious doubts on the decision taken by the Board of Crackwell Corporation?

(A) The Marketing Head is disliked by his team members because of his habit of criticising them in public

(B) Over the past three years, the profits of Crackwell's closest competitor have grown by 42% every year

(C) The CFO of Crackwell Corporation has taken several cost cutting measures over the last three years, including retrenchment of unproductive employees and renegotiation of prices with vendors.

(D) A strategy consulting firm, known to have turned around several poorly performing companies, has been recently hired by Crackwell Corporation

(E) Several new marketing campaigns, which gave a lot of international exposure to the company's products, have been successfully conducted by Crackwell Corporation over the past three years

Official Answer: C

Explanation

The argument suggests that the marketing head is the cause of the increase in profits over the last three years. To weaken this argument, we need to find an option that could provide an alternate explanation for this fact. (C) does this best by suggesting that the profits may have been increased because of the actions taken by the CFO and not the marketing head.

A. This doesn't take away from the fact that the marketing head could still be responsible for the increase in sales
B. The fact that Crackwell's competitor has performed better does not take away from the fact that Crackwell's profits have increased from 10% to 35%
C. The correct answer
D. The strategy consulting firm has only been hired recently whereas the profits of Crackwell have been increasing over the past three years
E. The credit for the successful marketing campaigns should obviously go to the marketing head, so this actually strengthens the argument.

79) In a recent survey of shoppers in the United States, 8 out of 10 shoppers said that they notice "Made in the USA" tags on products and most of those shoppers claim that they are more likely to purchase a product after noticing this tag. These shoppers further stated that the primary reason they are more likely to buy these products is because they wish to support the US economy.

Which of the following does most to show that the shoppers mentioned in the argument may have in fact been lying about why they purchase products with 'Made in America' labels?

(A) There is no difference in the quality of products manufactured in USA and those manufactured abroad

(B) The products that these shoppers said they would purchase include food, medicine, and personal items – products for the purchase of which quality and safety are the overriding considerations and in general products made in the USA are perceived to be safer than those made outside the USA

(C) Some customers purchase products with the "Made in USA" tag because they find the quality of these products to be better than those manufactured in other countries

(D) The products that are made in the USA in most cases cost significantly more than those manufactured abroad

(E) A large proportion of shoppers, who were not part of this survey, stated that when they buy a product they do not look at its country of manufacture

Official Answer: B

Explanation

Keep in mind that you don't need to weaken the fact that the shoppers in question don't buy products with "Made in the USA" tags. This is definitely true. What you need to question is whether the reason for buying these products is to help the country's economy. (B) does this best by stating that reason these shoppers could be buying these products is because they are safer and of better quality and not necessarily to help the economy.

A. This would ideally strengthen the argument and not weaken it. If the quality of the products is the same and shoppers are still buying those manufactured in USA, then they could be doing so to help the economy
B. The correct answer
C. While this option may appear similar to (B), it is in fact only talking about *some* customers. So some other customers could still be buying the products to help the economy
D. This could again strengthen the argument
E. Shoppers who were not part of this survey are outside the scope of the argument

80) Arguments to restrict immigration on the grounds that immigrants will take domestic jobs ignore the fact that immigrants, once employed, will earn and spend money on goods and services, creating new jobs that will more than make up for the old ones they took.

Which of the following is an assumption on which the argument depends?

(A) The immigrants will not send most of the money that they earn back to their hometowns

(B) Studies show that large scale inflow of immigrants invariably leads to an increase in the incidence of crime in that city

(C) The immigrants will not subsequently get their families to also join them in the new city

(D) Immigrants generally tend to save most of the money that they earn

(E) Opponents of immigration are not opposed to immigration for reasons other than loss of jobs

Official Answer: A

Explanation

The argument assumes that the immigrants will spend money in their city of immigration thereby helping create jobs in the city, but what if the immigrants don't do so? The argument obviously assumes that this will not be the case. (A) states this and is the assumption in the argument.

A. The correct answer
B. This is extra information and not an assumption
C. If the immigrants do so it will be a good thing because they will spend even more money in the new city
D. This would actually make the argument fall apart. The assumption has to be the opposite of this
E. The motives of the opponents of immigration are outside the scope of the argument

81) A subsidy is assistance paid to a business or an economic sector. Governments in developing countries provide subsidies to the general populace on several items such as fuel, cooking gas, etc. Of late such countries have faced a lot of criticism from the World Bank for continuing to offer these subsidies to their citizens. Nonetheless, given that elections are just around the corner in most of these countries, they are likely to continue offering these subsidies.

Which of the following inferences is best supported by the lines above?

(A) To win an election in a developing country, subsidies must be offered to the people

(B) Subsidies lead to inefficiencies in the economy of a nation

(C) Providing subsidies will improve the chances of the incumbent government coming back to power in the developing countries mentioned in the stimulus

(D) Developed countries do not provide any subsidies to their citizens

(E) Governments in developing countries favour appeasing people to achieving economic growth

Official Answer: C

Explanation

Since this is an Inference question, let's look at each option and eliminate.

A. The use of *must* makes this an extreme option. There could also be other ways of winning an election
B. Not necessarily. There could be some subsidies which could actually benefit the economy
C. The correct answer. If the reason for continuing to offer subsidies are elections, then there must be a causal link between the two
D. This cannot necessarily be concluded from the information in the stimulus
E. This is an extremely generalized statement which may or may not be true

82) Which of the following most logically completes the argument below?

Mobile phones emit radioactive radiation because they use radio frequency waves to make and receive calls. Even though the doses are very small, experts at the World Health Organisation (WHO) have voiced concern that these emissions might cause leukaemia and other diseases and have issued a warning against the excessive use of mobile phones. The WHO, then, is most likely going to issue a similar warning for home phones wired to a wall jack as well, because ________________ .

(A) home phones are also used to make and receive calls

(B) home phones are also communication devices used by the general public

(C) home phones also use radio frequency waves

(D) people, on an average, spend more time talking on home phones than on mobile phones

(E) experts have voiced concern about the use of home phones as well

Official Answer: C

Explanation

The word leading in to the blank is *because* which tells us that we need to strengthen the argument. The conclusion is the last sentence which states that WHO will issue a similar warning (to the one issued for mobile phone use) for home phones wired to a wall jack as well. The evidence clearly states that the problem with the use of mobile phones is that they emit radioactive radiation and the reason they emit radioactive radiation is because they use radio frequency waves. Thus (C) strengthens the argument by pointing out that home phones also use radio frequency waves and so will also emit harmful radioactive radiation.

A. This is not the reason why the warning has been issued against the excessive use of mobile phones
B. The problem is not with the function of the device but with its mode of communication (radio waves)
C. The correct answer
D. This may not necessarily be harmful if home phones do not emit radioactive radiation
E. But are they justified in doing so? This is the fact that we need to strengthen

83) **As pets have become increasingly humanised in recent years, almost becoming a substitute for children in some cases,** owners have become increasingly concerned about the quality of their pets' diets , leading to rising interest in grain-free offerings. **According to its critics, grain is merely a "filler" in pet food** that has little real nutritional benefit.

In the argument given, the two portions in boldface play which of the following roles?

(A) The first is the cause of a given effect; the second is a criticism of that effect

(B) The first is the cause of a given effect; the second is the opinion of a group that provides further support for this effect

(C) The first describes a general scenario and the second provides a specific implication of this scenario

(D) The first is the point of view of a group of people and the second contradicts this point of view by providing conflicting evidence

(E) The first is the conclusion of the argument and the second provides evidence on the basis of which this conclusion has been arrived at

Official Answer: B

Explanation

The argument states that as people are becoming more and more affectionate towards their pets, they are getting more and more concerned about their pets' diets. These people are looking at feeding their pets grain-free diets because grain apparently does not have any nutritional benefits. Both the first and the second bold parts provide reasons why people have become more averse to feeding their pets grain diets.

A. The first part could be true. The cause could be the pets getting humanized and the effect could be the desire of people to feed their pets grain-free diets. However the second bold part is not a criticism of that effect; it in fact supports that effect
B. This is the correct answer. The first part is the same as that of option A, and the second part further strengthens this fact
C. The first bold part could be a general scenario but the second bold part is definitely not an implication of this. The implication is actually the non-bold part in the middle of the argument
D. The first is not the point of view of any group and the second does not contradict it in any case
E. The first is not the conclusion of the argument; the conclusion is in the non bold part.

84) I do not think it is right to project electric cars as better than gas-fuelled cars. One negative aspect of electric cars is the fact they don't have enough power and, as a result, enough acceleration to perform in certain driving situations. For example, this lack of power could be dangerous in driving situations when fast acceleration is needed to avoid an accident.

Which of the following, if true, would most seriously weaken the argument above?

(A) Electric cars are much better for the ecology than are gas fuelled ones

(B) Electric cars are much cheaper to run than are gas fuelled cars

(C) The price of fuel is only expected to increase in the future whereas the price of technology used in the manufacture of electric cars is expect to decrease

(D) The biggest reason for road accidents is over speeding, which is the direct result of increased power in a car

(E) In future, electric cars are expected to have much more powerful engines than do current electric cars

Official Answer: D

Explanation

The argument assumes that there are no negatives associated with having a car with high power. (D) points out one such negative and thus weakens the argument

A. But the argument about electric cars lacking power and so being unsafe still stands
B. Same as (A)
C. Again the original problem still remains
D. The correct answer
E. If you go with this option, instead of weakening the argument, you are in fact agreeing with it and suggesting that this problem will most likely get rectified in the future.

85) Photon city is known for its commerce colleges across the nation. However, it seems that the quality of education imparted at these colleges has deteriorated considerably with time. When commerce graduates living in Photon city were recently administered a test, most of them could not even answer simple questions such as what was meant by activity based costing.

The argument is most vulnerable to the criticism that

(A) it incorrectly assumes that all commerce graduates have to be aware of what is meant by activity based costing

(B) it makes no distinction between commerce graduates living in Photon city and those who have graduated from commerce colleges in Photon city

(C) it does not take other important skills such as interpersonal skills and communication skills into consideration

(D) it provides no details about how commerce graduates in the rest of the country have performed on this test

(E) it does not take into account the education policies of the government

Official Answer: B

Explanation

The survey was conducted of commerce graduates living in Photon City; however there is nothing to suggest that all these students graduated from colleges in Photon City. If most of these students graduated from colleges outside Photon City, then it would not be fair to blame the colleges in Photon City for this fact. (B) raises this point and is the correct answer

A. The argument assumes no such thing. Activity based costing is just an example of simple questions that the graduates could not answer; the whole test was not about activity based costing
B. The correct answer
C. Other skills are outside the scope of the argument
D. We are only concerned with the situation in Photon City; what's happening in the rest of the county is irrelevant
E. Education policies of the government are outside the scope of the argument

86) The restrictions on what one can carry inside an airplane are surely too severe. Airlines these days issue a long checklist of items that cannot be carried inside an aircraft making it cumbersome for the travellers to keep a track of all these items. In any case barely two percent of travellers are ever caught with these restricted items, so it's best if these restrictions are removed.

Which of the following is an assumption on which the argument depends?

(A) The restrictions themselves do not discourage people from carrying restricted items on to airplanes

(B) The restrictions have been implemented all across the world

(C) There is no scope for corrupt practices on the part of those enforcing these restrictions

(D) There have been instances when an innocent traveller has been wrongly detained by over cautious airline personnel

(E) Criminals are hardly likely to carry restricted items with them on an airline

Official Answer: A

Explanation

The argument concludes that since only 2% of airline travellers are caught with restricted items, it doesn't make sense to have these restrictions in the first place. The argument assumes that it is not the restrictions themselves that prevent the other 98% of people from carrying restricted items on to airplanes.

A. The correct answer
B. This has no connection with the reasoning in the argument.
C. Whether there is scope for corruption on the part of those enforcing these restrictions is outside the purview of the argument
D. This could be an example of a problem with having the restrictions but is definitely not an assumption in the argument
E. This could be because of the restrictions; if the restrictions were not there the criminals would most likely carry such items with them on to airplanes

87) According to a research of 1000 individuals, 70% of the people who were part of Genco Slimming centre's weight loss program, lost an average of 4 pounds of weight in one month. However the same research also found that 80% of the people, who lost an average of 4 pounds of weight in that month, did not attend Genco Slimming centre's weight loss program.

Which of the following conclusions can most properly be drawn from the information above?

A. The number of people who were part of Genco's weight loss program is greater than the number of people who lost an average of more than 4 pounds of weight in that month

B. The people who did not join Genco's weight loss program and yet managed to lose an average of 4 pounds of weight in a month must have followed a very strict exercise regime of their own

C. The number of people who did not join Genco's weight loss program and who lost less than an average of 4 pounds of weight in the month is lower than the number of people who attended Genco's weight loss program and lost less than an average of 4 pounds of weight

D. The number of people who did not join Genco's weight loss program and who still managed to lose an average of more than 4 pounds of weight in that month is greater than the total number of people who joined Genco's weight loss program

E. The chances of a person losing an average of more than 4 pounds of weight in one month are higher if the person does not join Genco's weight loss program

Official Answer: D

Explanation: Since the argument contains a lot of figures, let's get a few things straight:

- We don't know how many of the 1000 people were part of Genco's weight loss program; we only know that 70% of this number were successful in losing an average of 4 pounds of weight in a month
- We also don't know the total number of people who lost an average of 4 pounds of weight in that month; we just know that 80% of these people did not attend Genco's weight loss program

From the above two statements we can definitely make out one thing – 20% of the people who lost an average of 4 pounds of weight in that month is equal to 70% of the people who were enrolled with Genco's weight loss program (since these people also lost an average of 4 pounds of weight in that month).

Let's assume the total number of people who enrolled at Genco's weight loss program be 100. Then those who lost an average of 4 pounds of weight = 70.

Now 70 is equal to 20% of the total number of people who lost an average of 4 pounds of weight. So the total number of people who lost an average of 4 pounds of weight = 350

Out of this 350, 280 were not enrolled with Genco's weight loss program. Thus it can be inferred that the number of people who did not join Genco's weight loss program and who still managed to lose more than 4 pounds of weight in that month is greater than the total number of people who joined Genco's weight loss program. (D) states this and is the correct answer.

A. This is statistically not possible, as described above
B. This may or may not have been the case. Maybe these people followed a very strict diet regime
C. We have no idea about how many people lost less than an average of 4 pounds of weight
D. The correct answer
E. Since the figure for the total number of people who enrolled for Genco's program is not provided to us, we cannot make any such inference

88) It appears that the residents of Clarktown are becoming more and more health conscious these days. The sale of fitness equipment such as treadmills and cycling machines has increased by more than 300% in Clarktown over the last one year.

Which of the following, if true, casts the most serious doubt on the conclusion drawn above?

(A) Due to a change in the sales tax structure last year, fitness equipment costs up to 30% less in Clarktown than in its neighbouring towns.

(B) The sale of health magazines has increased appreciably in Clarktown over the past one year.

(C) Nutritionists in Clarktown have reported a sharp increase in the cases of obesity that have been reported in Clarktown over the past year.

(D) The range of fitness equipment available at Clarktown is very limited and some advanced machines are not available at all

(E) Two athletes, both of whom won gold medals at the Olympics three years ago, are residents of Clarktown

Official Answer: A

Explanation

The argument assumes that most of the increase in sales of fitness equipment is on account of residents of Clarktown buying these. (A) weakens the argument by suggesting that, because the prices of fitness equipment in Clarktown are now lower, residents from the neighbouring towns might be the cause for this rapid increase in sales in the last one year. Thus the residents of Clarktown may not have been becoming more and more health conscious.

A. The correct answer
B. There could be several reasons for this. In any case this is not connected to the evidence used in the argument
C. Again this does not explain the 300% increase in the sales of fitness equipment
D. Irrelevant data
E. The athletes won the gold medal three years ago so why has the impact been felt only in the last year?

89) Researcher at Columbus Children's Hospital: **Migraines are common in children as are behavioural disorders such as attention deficit disorder (ADD), conduct disorder (CD) and oppositional defiant disorder (ODD).** We have now concluded that a direct relationship in fact exists between paediatric migraines and the behavioural disorder, ODD – one of the most common of the disruptive behavioural disorders occurring in children. **Children with migraines miss more school and often lose sleep,** factors which are known to contribute to the types of behavioural symptoms often associated with ODD,

In the argument given, the two portions in boldface play which of the following roles?

(A) The first is the main conclusion of the researcher and the second provides evidence supporting this main conclusion

(B) The first mentions terms, between the two of which the researcher later concludes exists a causal relation; the second is the basis for this conclusion

(C) The first is a general statement on the basis of which a conclusion is arrived at later in the argument; the second provides additional basis for this statement

(D) The first mentions terms, between the two of which the researcher later concludes exists a causal relation; the second is the basis for a secondary conclusion

(E) The first describes a possible correlation between migraine and certain other medical conditions and the second provides evidence suggesting that this correlation may in fact be a cause and effect relation

Official Answer: B

Explanation

In the argument, the researcher concludes that there is a causal relationship between migraine and ODD. The first bold part provides a general background and the second bold part helps explain the conclusion of the argument.

A. The first is not the main conclusion of the researcher. The main conclusion – that there is a causal link between migraine and ODD – is actually in the non bold part

B. The correct answer.
C. The first bold part can be described as a general statement but the conclusion is not arrived at on the basis of this statement. Also the second provides basis for the conclusion and not for this statement
D. While the first part is correct, the second bold part does not provide a basis for a secondary conclusion but for the main conclusion of the argument – that there is a causal link between migraine and ODD
E. The first could be correct but the second does not provide a causal link between migraine and all other disorders but only between migraine and ODD

90) 30% of the residents of Tafta City own cars. However 70% of the residents of Hampton, a suburb in Tafta City, are car owners. So it can be concluded that the total number of cars owned by residents of Hampton exceeds the total number of cars owned by the rest of the residents of Tafta City.

The answer to which of the following questions would be most important in determining whether the above conclusion is correct?

(A) What is the total population of Tafta City?

(B) What proportion of the population of Tafta City resides in Hampton?

(C) What is the total number of cars owned by residents of Tafta City?

(D) What is the total number of people residing in Hampton?

(E) What proportion of the population of Tafta City has bought cars from outside Tafta City?

Official Answer: B

Explanation

The argument only provides us with percentages; it never gives us any absolute number. We know that 30% of the total residents of Tafta City own cars but we don't what is this number. Again we know that 70% of the residents of Hampton own cars, but we don't know what proportion of the total population of Tafta City are these residents.

Say the total population of Tafta City is 100. Out of these 30 people own cars. Now let's look at two possibilities:

Possibility 1: 20% of the population of Tafta City lives in Hampton. So the total number of cars in Hampton is 14, whereas the total number of cars owned by the rest of the residents of Tafta City is (30-14) = 16. Thus the conclusion of the argument is NOT true.

Possibility 2: 30% of the population of Tafta City lives in Hampton. So the total number of cars in Hampton is 21, whereas the total number of cars owned by the rest of the residents of Tafta City is (30-21) = 9. Thus the conclusion of the argument IS true.

So to evaluate whether the conclusion of the argument is true or not, we need to know what proportion of the population of Tafta City resides in Hampton. (B) states this and is the correct answer.

A. Knowing the total population will not help unless we know the proportion that stays in Hampton
B. The correct answer
C. Knowing the total number of cars does not help unless you know what proportion of these are in Hampton
D. This may look tempting but will not help unless you know what percentage of the population of Tafta City is this number
E. Irrelevant fact

91) For people looking at purchasing laptops, there are two important decision parameters – the speed of the laptop's processor and the backup that its battery provides. Jake, an expert at computers, believes that, of the two determinants, processor speed is the more important one. Surprisingly he recommends that his friends buy the laptop with the longest battery backup.

Which of the following best explains the apparent contradiction between Jake's belief and his recommendation?

(A) Jack is aware that a laptop with a processor that is faster than any of the current processors will be launched within the next six months

(B) Jake is aware that for a lot of buyers, a third factor – the weight of the laptop – is more important than the other two factors

(C) All the laptops currently available in the market use the same processor

(D) Laptops with powerful batteries cost more than those with regular batteries

(E) Jake is probably not as much of an expert at computers as he likes to believe

Official Answer: C

Explanation

The only way to explain this fact is by assuming that out of the two factors in question, one is constant. In that case is makes sense to maximize the other factor. (C) states that all the laptops in the market have the same processor, then it makes sense to buy the one with the longest battery backup.

A. If this was the case Jack should have advised his friends to not buy a laptop at all for the next six months

B. The presence of a third factor is outside the scope of the argument
C. The correct answer
D. Does not explain the contradiction in the stimulus
E. The stimulus clearly states that Jack is an expert at computers

92) It is truly a waste of time to attend college. Out of the ten richest people in the world at the moment, six are college dropouts. Thus, if one wants to become rich, then it makes sense to drop out of college and start one's own venture.

Which of the following, if true, casts the most serious doubt on the argument?

(A) Had the six people mentioned in the argument attended college, they may have been even richer than they are currently

(B) Attending college helps a person increase his or her social circle by making new friends

(C) Statistics reveal that 95% of all new ventures are most likely to fail

(D) The percentage of college dropouts who have gone on to become rich is several times smaller than the percentage of college graduates who have gone on to become rich

(E) Becoming rich is not the only measure of success, happiness is perhaps more important

Official Answer: D

Explanation

The argument assumes that the probability of a college dropout succeeding is higher than that of a college graduate. However, this fact can only be properly ascertained if we knew how many of the total college dropouts have gone on to become successful or rich and how many of the college graduates have done so. (D) uses this point to highlight the fact that the chances of a college graduate becoming rich are much higher than those of a college drop out.

A. The six people are already the richest in the world; whether they could get even richer is not relevant to the argument. What is relevant is whether a high percentage of other college dropouts can also become as rich as these six people.

B. Social circle is outside the scope of the argument

C. This is an irrelevant fact because this is true for both college dropouts and college graduates

D. The correct answer

E. The argument is only concerned about becoming rich so this option is outside the scope

93) Over the last few years that he has been travelling by the subway, Ricky has made an interesting observation. Every time the train is late by more than six minutes, it gets extremely crowded and Ricky finds it impossible to get a seat. In the last 6 years, it has never happened that the train arrived more than six minutes late and Ricky could find a place to sit.

Which of the following conclusions can most properly be drawn from the above statements?

(A) The number of people travelling by the subway has increased several times over the last few years

(B) If the train comes on time, Ricky will definitely get a place to sit

(C) If Ricky does not find a seat in the train, it must have arrived more than six minutes late

(D) The Transport Authority needs to urgently increase the frequency of subway trains

(E) If the train arrives more than six minutes late, Ricky will most likely not find a place to sit

Official Answer: E

Explanation

The stimulus states that if the train comes more than 6 minutes late, Ricky will most likely not find a seat. Don't use this fact to conclude that the opposite will also be true – that if Ricky does not find a place to sit, then the train must have come six minutes late. There could be other reasons for this as well.

A. No such inference can be made from the argument
B. Again this does not have to be necessarily true
C. Incorrect as explained above
D. No such inference can be made from the argument
E. The correct answer

94) The number of people in Denvo city who like to watch movies in multiplexes has apparently increased considerably. Over the last five years it has become difficult to find seats in most multiplexes in Denvo City.

Which of the following, if true, most seriously weakens the argument?

(A) Several blockbuster movies were released in the last five years

(B) Denvo city had seven multiplexes out of which three have shut down in the last five years

(C) Many residents of Denvo city have stated in a survey that they hate going out for movies.

(D) The ticket prices charged by multiplexes in Denvo city have fallen over the past five years

(E) It is very easy to find seats in multiplexes situated in the neighbouring Vento city

Official Answer: B

Explanation

The argument suggests that the reason it is difficult to find seats in multiplexes in Denvo City is because of the increase in the number of viewers. However (B) questions this fact by stating that the number of multiplexes has gone down by almost fifty percent, so the number of viewers could have remained unchanged and yet it would become difficult to find seats because the number of seats itself has gone down.

A. This provides an explanation for the situation described in the argument and does not weaken it.

B. The correct answer

C. If this is so then why has it become difficult to find seats?

D. Same as (A)

E. The situation in some other city is irrelevant to the argument

95) Researchers have long been trying to understand why the consumption of opium makes one sleepy. A group of researchers has recently concluded that opium is sleep inducing because it has soporific qualities.

Which of the following parallels the flaw in the reasoning above?

(A) The student performed poorly in the test because he did not study for it

(B) It is dark at night because of the absence of the sun

(C) The new car has a powerful engine so it must also have powerful brakes

(D) Aeroplanes are able to fly because of their aerodynamic shape

(E) The price of a company' stock has not appreciated because the company's stock price has remained stagnant

Official Answer: E

Explanation

This is an example of an argument which takes the conclusion as one of its premises. Such arguments usually make use of synonyms such as 'sleep inducing' and 'soporific'. The two mean the same so the argument never really explains why opium is sleep inducing. (E) repeats this fallacy by stating that a stock price has not appreciated because it has remained stagnant (which is the same thing). But why has this stock price not appreciated? This option never answers this question.

A. This is a direct cause and effect relation
B. Same as (A)
C. This is an illogical conclusion but does not parallel the reasoning in the original argument
D. Again a direct cause and effect relation
E. The correct answer

96) Banker: Our asset quality is fairly strong and has been improving in the past few quarters. But given our size, we cannot afford to allow any of our large accounts to turn non-performing. It would create havoc for us.

Which of the following must be true on the basis of the statements made by the banker above?

(A) The bank in questions must be a small sized bank

(B) If any of the bank's accounts become non performing, the bank will go bankrupt

(C) The bank does not mind if any of its smaller accounts turn non-performing

(D) The bank used to have assets of a poor quality a few quarters back

(E) One of the important factors that will determine the bank's performance is the quality of its large accounts

Official Answer: E

Explanation

Since this is an Inference question, let's look at each option and eliminate

A. There is no way of concluding this
B. This is an extreme conclusion. While we know in such a case the bank will be negatively affected, we can't necessarily conclude that the bank will go bankrupt
C. Again this doesn't necessarily have to be true. This may not impact the bank as much as the non-performance of a large account would, but it might still be a bad thing for the bank
D. That the asset quality of the bank has improved does not necessarily mean its asset quality was poor a few quarters back. Maybe it was good then and has become even better now
E. This has to be true because the stimulus clearly states that even if one large account goes bad the bank will face problems. So while there could very well be other factors that affect the bank's performance, the quality of its large accounts definitely has to be one of them.

97) Opponents of the free market approach assert that the free market often fails to achieve maximum efficiency—that it sometimes wastes resources. They often cite the example of utility services. If there were free competition among utilities, it would lead to a lot of duplication—different companies putting up telephone and electric poles, waterlines, etc., side by side, which would be a waste. So they argue that it is important for government to restrict competition and thus correct market failures.

The answer to which of the following questions would help evaluate whether the opponents of free market theory are correct?

(A) Whether it is possible to procure items such as electric and telephone poles used by utility services at low prices

(B) Whether there is some other feasible way of solving the problem of duplication mentioned in the argument

(C) Whether following this strategy is likely to lead to formation of monopolies that can be then used to exploit consumers

(D) Whether free market is likely to have any detrimental effect on the economy of the country

(E) Whether the free market approach has been adopted by any other countries in the world

Official Answer: C

Explanation

The argument is assuming that there will be no negative aspects of restricting competition. But what if restricting competition gave rise to monopolies? Then there could be negative consequences of this move. (C) addresses this point and is the correct answer

A. Even if these items can be procured at low prices, why spend money on duplication?
B. We are only concerned about the method described in the argument; any other methods are outside the scope
C. The correct answer
D. Even if the free market does not have a detrimental effect on the economy of a country, it does not necessarily mean that it will have a beneficial effect either
E. What has happened in other countries is outside the scope of the argument

98) A proposal has recently been floated by the government to increase road use tax rates across the country. This will lead to an increase in operating costs for trucking companies, who will then most likely increase their freight rates. The higher freight rates will in turn lead to a consequent increase in the prices of goods and commodities of daily use such as vegetable and grocery items. Thus if the proposal is passed, it will actively contribute to inflation in the country.

Which of the following, if true, most strongly indicates that the logic of the prediction above is flawed?

(A) It assumes that there is no other way in which inflation can increase apart from increased road use taxes

(B) It mistakes a likely outcome for a confirmed outcome

(C) It resorts to addressing peripheral issues while ignoring the deeper fundamental problems with the economy

(D) It assumes that the inflation will not increase if the road tax is not increased

(E) It mistakes a correlation for a cause and effect relation

Official Answer: B

Explanation

Notice that the argument states that trucking companies will *most likely* increase their freight rates. *Most likely* does not mean that this will definitely happen. Trucking companies may have already built this increase in road use tax into their current prices, in which case they will not increase the freight rates. Then the entire argument will fall apart. So the flaw in the argument is that it assumes that a likely outcome will be a definite outcome i.e. (B) is the correct answer.

A. The argument assumes no such thing. As long as increase in freight rates can be one cause of inflation, the argument will hold true
B. The correct answer
C. The argument does no such thing
D. The argument does not assume this
E. There is no mention of correlation in the argument. The argument only talks about cause and effect relations. The question is whether this cause and effect will definitely take place?

99) Board of ABC Company: Owing to the excellent performance of the company in the last four quarters under the leadership of the new CEO, the Board has decided to reward the CEO with a 50% bonus.

Shareholder of ABC Company: But last year ABC Company's sales grew by only 30%, which was the lowest amongst all its competitors.

Which of the following provides the most logical counter for the Board to offer to the shareholder?

(A) ABC Company's sales had fallen every year for the past three years

(B) The CEO cannot be personally held responsible for the low sales growth

(C) The CEO needs to be encouraged, else he may lose the motivation to increase the sales further

(D) The CEO has hired several middle managers at very high salaries leading to increased costs for the company

(E) The CEO has not made any remarkable changes to the production or marketing strategy of the company

Official Answer: A

Explanation

In this argument we need to strengthen the Board's decision and at the same time also explain how the fact that the company's sales have only grown by 30% is not necessarily a bad thing. (A) does this by pointing out that ABC's sales had been continuously falling for the past three years, so if the sales this year have shown a 30% growth then, in relative terms, this performance is very good.

A. The correct answer
B. But then there is no reason to reward the CEO either
C. The encouragement cannot be at the cost of falling sales. If the growth rate of the company's sales has fallen down compared to the previous years, then there is no reason to reward the CEO
D. This weakens the argument of the Board by suggesting that the CEOs policies could lead to increase in costs
E. Same as (D)

100) In a college election Tom received 50% of the votes cast, Jim received 30% of the votes cast, and Joanna received the remaining 20% of the votes cast. Jim was eventually declared the winner of the election for the post of the college President.

Which of the following conclusions can most properly be drawn from the information above?

(A) There were only three candidates who stood for the election

(B) The college students most likely don't like Joanna

(C) Tom must have spent more time campaigning than Jim or Joanna did

(D) The number of votes received was not a criterion to decide who would be President

(E) There must be some criterion, other than the number of votes received, that also helps decide who would be President

Official Answer: E

Explanation

Since this is an Inference question, let's look at each option and eliminate

A. This may not necessarily be the case. There could be a fourth candidate (or even more than four) who did not receive any votes
B. There is no way of arriving at this conclusion
C. Same as (B)
D. Extreme option. We know that the number of votes received could not have been the only criterion, in which case Tom would have won, but this does not necessarily mean that this was not a criterion at all.
E. The correct answer. If Jim won despite not receiving the maximum number of votes, then there has to be some factor other than the number of votes received that helps decide who would be President

PART 5

Quick Recall

The purpose of this section is to give you all the important rules/concepts discussed in this book in one place. Go through this section before you take a full length practice test so that all the *critical* aspects of Critical Reasoning are fresh in your mind.

Basics of Critical Reasoning

- Every CR Question has three parts – Stimulus, Question Stem, Options
- Stimulus can appear in two forms – Argument & Statements of facts
- Assumption + Evidence = Conclusion
- Conclusion
    - Gives the answer to *What* the author is saying
    - Almost always an opinion
    - Can appear anywhere in an argument (not necessarily at the end)
- Evidence
    - Gives the answer to *Why* the author is saying what he is saying
    - Almost always contains facts
    - Can never be questioned or doubted. Always take it at face value
- Assumption
    - Is unstated evidence
    - Must be true for the argument to be true
- Approach to Critical Reasoning
    - Start by reading the stimulus and not the question stem
    - Read the stimulus critically and summarize it in your own words
    - Read the Question stem and use the strategy to tackle that particular question type
    - Take an average of two minutes to answer each CR question

Assumption Questions

- Assumption is the most important of all CR concepts
- Assumption helps answer five questions types
    - *Find an Assumption*
    - *Evaluate the Argument*
    - *Strengthen*
    - *Weaken*
    - *Identify the Flaw*
- Assumption will never be written in the argument

- Never question the argument's conclusion, however absurd
- Always predict the assumption before looking at the options
- Try the Denial/Negation rule if confused between options
- Active Assumptions
    - Actively support the argument
    - Can be pre-phrased or predicted in advance
    - Usually an argument has only one Active Assumption
- Passive Assumptions
    - Cannot be predicted because there can be several in an argument
    - Always use some negating word such as *not*
- Assumption questions can also be worded as *must be true* questions

Evaluate the Argument Questions

- Stimulus will be in the form of an argument
- Indirectly require you to identify the Assumption
- The correct option will strengthen the argument (if the option is true) and weaken the argument (if the option is false)
- Options start with the word *whether* or are worded in the form of questions

Strengthen Questions

- The stimulus will always be in the form of an argument
- Strengthener will make it more likely for the conclusion to be arrived at from the evidence
- Never strengthen just the conclusion in isolation. Always strengthen the link between the evidence and the conclusion
- A lot of times the answer to a Strengthen question is the Assumption itself
    - Assumption always strengthens the argument
- Active strengtheners provide a point in favour of the argument
- Passive strengtheners remove a doubt about the argument
    - Will use the word *not*

Weaken Questions

- The stimulus will always be in the form of an argument
- Weaken will make it less likely for the conclusion to be arrived at from the evidence

- Never weaken just the conclusion in isolation. Always weaken the link between the evidence and the conclusion
- The answer to a Weaken question will raise doubts about the validity of the assumption

Identify the Flaw Questions

- The flaw will always question the assumption
- Stimulus will be in the form of an argument
- Can also be worded as *vulnerable to the objection* or *vulnerable to the criticism* questions
- Different from Weaken questions
    - Flaw is always from within the argument
    - Weaken always provides additional evidence against the argument
- Typical Flaws
    - Mistaking Correlation for Causation
    - Confusing you with Absolute Numbers and Percentages
    - Representativeness

Inference Questions

- Stimulus will usually not be in the form of an argument
- You are not required to summarize the information in the stimulus
- The correct option *must* be true and not *may* be true
- Can be worded as *must be true* questions or *support* questions
- Don't try to predict the answer
- Look at each option and eliminate
- Always avoid extreme or strongly worded options
- Never use outside information to answer Inference questions
- Assumptions usually play no role in Inference questions

Explain Questions

- Stimulus will always contain a discrepancy/anomaly/contradiction
- Any option that explains this contradiction will be the correct answer
    - Will always be a new point containing extra outside information
- Always explain both sides of the contradiction and not just one side
- Never question or deny the contradiction or the evidence

Provide a Logical Conclusion Questions

- Always have a blank at the end
- Increasingly tested on the GMAT
- Stimulus will usually be in the form of an argument
- Most questions will require you to strengthen the conclusion. The conclusion is in the sentence that leads to the blank.
- The word leading into the blank will tell you what question type to treat the questions as.
    - Since/because – Strengthen question
    - It should be expected that – Inference question
    - Assuming that – Assumption question

Miscellaneous Questions

- Bold faced Questions
    - Always paraphrase the argument and predict the relation between the two bold parts before looking at the options
    - Remember to answer only for the bold part
    - Instead of selecting the correct option, try eliminating the incorrect ones
- Main Point Questions
    - The correct answer will not just restate the conclusion; it will also incorporate parts of the evidence
    - Avoid answers which summarise only a part of the argument or which restate a fact from the argument
- Parallel Reasoning Questions
    - The options will always be from diverse fields that have no apparent connection with what is mentioned in the stimulus
    - The exact structure of the correct answer may not be the same as that of the argument.
    - Watch out for options that are half-right and half-wrong

Common Argument Structures

- Cause and Effect Argument
    - If the argument states that A is causing B, then there are two ways of weakening this:
        - Show that C could also cause B
        - Show that it is actually B that might be causing A

- Representativeness
    - Whenever the argument talks about a survey, research, study, etc. always check for the error of Representativeness
- Number Arguments
    - A higher percentage could lead to a lower number and vice versa
    - A higher number could lead to a lower percentage and vice versa
    - For any number argument question you need three details – the total number, the absolute number and the percentage
    - If the stimulus contains percentages, avoid answer choices that contain absolute numbers
    - If the stimulus contains absolute numbers, avoid answer choices that contain percentages

Important Terms on GMAT Critical Reasoning

- Options containing terms such as *some* and *many* will rarely be correct
- Prefer options with terms such as *most* and *majority*
- If the option contains the word *not*, it might be a passive assumption or a passive strengthener
- Pay attention to the use of EXCEPT
- If four options strengthen the argument, it is not necessary that the fifth will weaken it

Concluding Notes:

Through this book we have endeavoured to provide you with all the Critical Reasoning concepts tested on the GMAT in one place. This book has been written in a lucid, easy to understand style; in fact we have made a conscious effort to avoid diagrams and jargon as much as possible and focus on understanding the meaning of arguments instead.

While we have tried to ensure that the book is completely free of errors, in case you do spot one please post it on the CR Grail thread on the Forums section of our website. Also in case there are some concepts that you could not understand from the book or that you would like to discuss with us, please post the same on our forums and we'll respond to you within 48 hours.

We also welcome any other feedback that you may have on how we can make the next edition of this book even better; do mail us the same on feedback@aristotleprep.com

We wish you all the best for your preparation.

The CR Grail Editorial Team

If you found this book useful, do check out the other book in our Grail series:

The SC Grail 3rd Edition

Here are some standout features of the SC Grail:

- Covers the entire gamut of concepts tested on GMAT Sentence Correction, from the most basic ones to the more advanced ones
- Helps you master sentence correction in a step-by-step manner.
- Provides Targeted Practice drills at the end of each chapter for conceptual clarity
- Does not just give pages of theory but also helps you understand how a concept is tested on actual GMAT questions by referencing the Official Guide for GMAT Review 13th or the 12th edition whenever necessary
- Devotes an entire section to what the GMAT likes and dislikes between two options such as *whether and if, like and as, will and would*, etc.

CPSIA information can be obtained at www.ICGtesting.com
Printed in the USA
LVOW091955210113

316600LV00030B/2620/P

9 789350 872857